FOOTSTEPS OF THE SAINTS

THE CHILDREN OF THE PROMISE

—

BASED ON
A MANUAL OF CHURCHHISTORY
By A. H. Newman

—

Presented by Almon Teel

Copyright © 2012, by A.B. Teel, Merced, Ca

This book is dedicated to the untold numbers of the faithful, in all ages, who paid a dear price to light a candle in the darkness.

TO SELF-APPOINTED JUDGES AND SEEKERS OF REVENGE

    Making the world free from barbaric laws and customs has been a slow process. Calls for revenge, which should have vanished long ago from this earth, still exist, as some, who feel less compelled to do good than to execute judgment upon others, take the law into their own hands. They say they are standing up for God, or standing up for Jesus. Al Gore, former Vice-President of the United States has been quoted as saying, "Killing in the name of religion goes on all over the world." We can only hope that those of such passions can be reminded that the Lord said, "Vengeance is mine," and that retribution will be left in His hands.

TABLE OF CONTENTS

Preface..vii
Acknowledgements..................................viii
Prologue..ix

PART I...1
   On a Road Leading to Rome

PART II...37
   Through the Long Dark Night

PART III 85
   Toward the Light of the Dawn

PART IV..117
   Revolution and Reform

Postscript...181
Bibliography..183

BIBLE QUOTATIONS

The Bible may be quoted in either the American Standard Version, 1901 (ASV), or the King James Version (KJV); otherwise, it is paraphrased.

PREFACE

Footsteps of the Saints is based on Professor A. H. Newman's comprehensive, two-volume, *A Manual of Church History* which "grew out of his own needs as a teacher. It is "primarily intended as a textbook for theological seminaries and universities," but is felt it to be "equally adapted to the needs of ministers of the gospel and of intelligent laymen." The hope for *Footsteps of the Saints* is much the same, except that as a simpler version it will read more widely, that a greater part of the population might come to a better understand of The Christianity of Christ.

A primary objective for *Footsteps of the Saints* is far from merely cataloging events of the past. It shows the effects of Scriptural interpretations, theological concepts, greed, and all manner of human motivations found on the pathway – whether of children of God or imposters in the Faith For example, the fanatic Thomas Munzer, who in Swabia, in 1525, believing the Old Testament to be a literal guide for Christians, imposed himself as a leader in an uprising of the peasants against their lords. As he was convinced "the sword of Gideon was in his hands," he led a host of peasants upon the castles of their lords which they held responsible for their suppression. "On, on, on," he shouted; "slay, slay, slay, and tire not; nevermind the wail of the godless."

Newman comments: "Alas, for the church of Christ if it should ever come to look upon the sword of Gideon as a fit instrument for the setting up of the kingdom of God, or to conceive of the Christ of God as leading a carnal host to the slaughter of the ungodly."

Acknowledgement of

THE WORK OF A. H. NEWMAN

A Manual of Church History, Dr. A.H. Newman, D.D., LL.D., was first published by the American Baptist Publication Society (Volume I in 1899 and Volume II in 1902). The two-volume history, followed by a revised and enlarged edition in 1933, has been reprinted many times by Judson Press for use in theological institutions.

Dr. Newman was one of the first two professors placed on the staff during the opening year of Baylor University's Theological Department, which a few years later separated from Baylor and became Southwestern Baptist Theological Seminary. Already a well-recognized church historian, Newman's addition to the staff brought "instant credibility to the institution," according to an article in the May/June 1993 issue of *Southwestern News*, A publication of Southwestern Baptist Theological Seminary.

Newman, held the chair of Professor of Church History in Rochester Theological Seminary 1877-1881, McMaster Univ. 1881-1901, Baylor Univ. 1901-1907 and 1913-1921, Southwestern Baptist Theological Seminary 1907-1913, and Mercer Univ. 1921-1929. He served as guest professor at the University of Chicago 1906-1926, Vanderbilt University 1917 and 1918, and McMaster University 1927-1929. He held membership in several historical societies and was Vice-president of The American Baptist Historical Society.

PROLOGUE

Footsteps of the Saints traces the journey of Christianity from the purity of the teachings of Christ to the pinnacle of prestige and power, then follows its course through the long night of the Dark Ages; Its roots, however run deep into Abraham's native land and through the lands of his wonderings.

∞

Ur, was a city-state in ancient Sumer where it was a custom to bring offerings and sacrifices to an altar or shrine to appease the oft-times angry or capricious gods. They, like most ancient civilizations, recognized a special status for the prominent figures of creation, such as the sun, the moon, the stars, and kings and heroes that seemed to dominate the earth and sky. Changes in the looks of the heavens reflected the disposition of the gods, and the stars and constellations of stars showed their prowess when the sky was dark, and they took prominent places on the astrological schematics of virtually every society.

Two thousand years before Abraham, the gods were innumerable. They were all honored throughout the land, but every city had its own supreme patron, or city god, who was the owner and priest of the principal temple, lord of the land, governor of the state, and leader of the host in time of war. The God of all Gods was unknown. The human ruler, "patesi" (governor or king), was simply the representative of the supreme patron god of each city.

All other gods had their normal functions. They could be lord of the wind, the rain, earthquakes, love, the plague, childbirth or whatever the situation demanded, for even "ancient legends might be modified to suit the local cult." But those gods were little more than attendants to the city god, whose position was set so high as to be unapproachable by mere man, so those who brought petitions would usually choose the minor deities to mediate between themselves and the city god.

Daily public sacrifices consisted of ordinary meals that were shared by the priests and workers in the temple. A large number of animals would be used, with certain parts reserved for the god (the city god, who owned the temple). Illusion and charm were used by the priests to prompt the god to exercise his power in a favorable manner.

Private sacrifices were offered to secure an answer to prayer or petition, for example, for a person to regain his health. Much magic and little religion was involved as bread, wine, honey, and spices were set out before the statue of the god, alongside an animal for the offering. The animal, typically, a lamb, would be dismembered and the god of the temple would be given his prescribed portion.

Parts of the lamb would be laid out on the corresponding parts of the petitioner's body, and the rest of it would be shared with participants in the rite. The liturgy explained that the lamb was a substitute for the petitioner, and that its life would be offered to give life to him in its stead. Excavations of the gravesites at Ur have revealed that human sacrifice was used in the case of a life for life offering for the king.[1]

∞

---

[1] C. Leonard Woolley, The Sumerians, New York: W.W. Norton & Co.), pp. 90-129

Somewhere amidst the magic spells and illusions of the sacrificial offerings to the temple gods, Abraham heard the voice of the One and Only, Righteous, Loving, True and Living God, who would call upon Abraham to follow Him and lead his people to higher, more honorable, and loving ways of human behavior.

And God said unto Abraham (Paraphrasing): I want you to get out of your country and away from your kindred. I want you to go to a land that I will show you. I will make of you a great nation, and your name shall be great. I will bless those who bless you and curse those who curse you, for in you and your seed shall all nations of the earth be blessed.[2] Abraham believed in Jehovah, and it was counted to him for righteousness.[3]

Abraham set out on his journey, and God, in His own time, would provide the lessons for the learning. Abraham had not been in Canaan long when he was given the opportunity to pay tithes to Melchisedec, "Priest of God Most High,[4] like unto the Son of God."[5] Not like any priest known in his native land. He foreshadowed the great high priest that was to come, as was said of Him: He came "after the order of Melchisedek."[6]

As Abraham grew older, and Sarah was past childbearing age, he became concerned that he did not have a son. Didn't God say, "I will make of thee a great nation?" What was he supposed to do? He and his wife, Sarah fell back on ancient custom and gave Hagar, her bondmaid in her place. Consequently Abraham was given a son by Hagar.

---

[2] Genesis 12.1-3
[3] Gen. 15.6 (ASV)
[4] Gen. 14.18 (ASV)
[5] Heb. 7.3 (ASV)
[6] Heb. 7-17 (ASV)

God was not through, however, for he promised that Sarah, too, would have a child. She laughed, and ridiculed the thought, because she would be 90 years of age and Abraham would be 100. Nevertheless, she miraculously gave birth to Isaac. Abraham, now, has two sons, one by Hagar, the bondmaid, and the other by Sarah, his wife.

The Apostle Paul, our greatest Bible commentator, had reason to comment on this story, for in his absence from the churches in Galatia, some Jewish Christians, known as Judaizers, were stirring up the new Gentile Christians, telling them that they would have to become Jews, obey all the laws of the Jews, and carry on all Jewish traditions before they could become Christians.

Paul, then, by way of the letter to the Galatians, set the matter straight by referring them the story of Abraham as set forth in the Scriptures, and he said, "These things are an allegory."[7] "Scripture, foreseeing that God would justify the Gentiles by faith, preached the Gospel beforehand unto Abraham, saying, "In thee shall all nations be blessed. So, then, they that are of faith are blessed with faithful Abraham."[8]

Paul explained, (paraphrasing): Abraham had two sons, one by the handmaid and one by the freewoman. The son of the handmaid came by natural birth, but the son of the freewoman was born miraculously according to the promise.[9] The two women represent two mountains, two covenants and two cities. Hagar is Mount Sinai, in Arabia, bearing children into bondage under the law, and corresponds to the Jerusalem that is now, for

---

[7] Galatians 4.24 (Pharaphrased)
[8] Gal. 3.8-9 (ASV)
[9] Gal. 4.22-23 (Paraphrased)

she is in bondage with her children.[10] Sarah, however, is a free woman, and her children are free. She represents Mount Moriah, the mountain of grace, and the Jerusalem, above, which is free.[11]

Paul wrote to those who had fallen under the spell of the Judaizers, "I marvel that ye are so quickly removed from Him that called you in the grace of Christ unto another gospel,"[12] only It was not another gospel. "False brethren ... came in privily to spy out our liberty which we have in Christ Jesus they might bring us into bondage."[13]

He had a question for the new Christians: "Having begun in the spirit, are you now made perfect by the flesh?"[14] (Are you now going to depend on perfect obedience to the law and the performance of ceremonial duties to make you perfect)?

Tell me, he said, to those who desired to be under the law: (Paraphrasing) Do you know anything about the law?[15] (The centerpiece of the ceremonial law, or the Covenant of Mount Sinai is the "Little Book of the Covenant," found in Exodus, just after the Ten Commandments.)[16]

(The Jews also find 613 laws in the Book of the Law, which is Genesis through Deuteronomy, which must be obeyed. In addition, the recorded comments of the temple priests and many symbolic gestures, such as touching, are just as binding to the Jews as the laws, themselves.)[17]

---

[10] Gal. 4.24-25 (ASV)
[11] Gal. 4.26 (ASV)
[12] Gal. 1.6 (ASV)
[13] Gal. 2.4 (ASV)
[14] Gal. 3.3 (Paraphrased)
[15] Gal.4.21 (Paraphrased)
[16] Exodus, Chapters 21-23
[17] www.jewfac.org

Paul said to his deceived converts: They that are of faith are blessed with faithful Abraham. Christ redeemed us from the curse of the law, having become a curse for us, that the blessing of Abraham in Christ Jesus might come upon the Gentiles, that we might become children of the promise through faith, "but those that are under the works of the law are under a curse, for it is written, cursed is everyone who fails to do all the things that are written in the book of the law.[18]

∞

The Jews misunderstood the purpose and the power of the law. The law is "a shadow of the good things to come,"[19] but has no power to justify[20] or to make things whole. The law was given to teach.[21] It reveals what is wrong and then condemns it. The offering of sacrifices year after year brings about a remembrance of sin, but no matter how sincere the expectations, or how intense the performance of the duties, the requirements of the law can never be satisfied and "make the comers thereunto perfect."[22] "For by grace are ye saved through faith; and that not of yourselves: it is the gift of God: not of works, lest any man should boast."[23]

Just as the Jews misunderstood the law, they misunderstood the prophecies of the coming of the Messiah. They expected the Messiah to appear suddenly, in miraculous displays of power to overthrow the enemies of Israel and the hosts of evil. The idea of a suffering Savior, as portrayed by the prophet Isaiah,[24] had little place

---

[18] Gal. 3.10-14
[19] Heb. 10.1 (Paraphrased)
[20] Acts 13.39
[21] Gal. 3.24
[22] Heb. 10.1 (KJV)
[23] Ephesians 2 8-9 (KJV)
[24] Is. 53.1-12

in the Jewish thought of the time, but Jesus, the Christ, when He came, made it clear that he would not overthrow the hosts of evil and drive away the enemies of Israel from the face of the earth. His kingdom was "not of this world." His kingdom was a kingdom "within."

W. T. Conner, referring to the story of the Hebrew people, writes: "The Old Testament theocracy finds its whole significance in relation to the spiritual kingdom for which it was a providential preparation." and he calls it a paradox that "through the rejection of this Messiah by Israel, He became a spiritual King for the whole (human) race, ruling by the power of redeeming love, all who accept him."[25].

For the last 200 years, in America, we and our fathers have joined our great grandfathers in "preaching the gospel" through the singing of the pleas, the praises, and battle cries of the Hebrews in such songs as "Back to Bethel," "Let My People Go," "I am Bound For the Promised Land," and "I Won't Have To Cross Jordan Alone," "There's a Land Beyond the River," We're Marching to Zion," and "The Pearly White City," along with the many other songs of praise and petition that were printed in our hymnbooks.

We sang in celebration of the love of God, for His goodness and mercy, for salvation, and the freedom we share; we celebrated the nation through whom was born the salvation of the humankind; we celebrated the Old Testament, called "Scripture" in the time of the apostles, centered about the law, the Ten Commandments, and the "Old Covenant." Scripture contains the wonderful stories and writings of wisdom and beauty throughout; but it is also contains the history of Gods dealings with the Hebrew nation in times when God still had lessons

---

[25] W. T. Conner, *The Gospel of Redemption,* p.292

for their learning. This was in the "times of ignorance," when men compared God to their carvings of silver and gold, and He "winked at"[26] (or overlooked) their sin.

The Old Testament prophesied the coming of the New Covenant. Jeremiah wrote: "Behold the days come," saith the Lord, "that I will make a new covenant with the house of Israel, and with the house of Judah:"[27] "Not according to the covenant that I made with their fathers in the day when I took them by the hand to bring them out of the land of Egypt; which my covenant they brake,... I will put my law in their inward parts, and write it in their hearts; and I will be their God and they shall be my people...."[28] Not a kingdom postponed,[29], but a kingdom "within."[30]

"God closed the eyes of the Jews so they could not see, and their ears so they could not hear; and they stumbled that the Gentiles might receive Salvation."[31] "And they, also, if they continue not in their unbelief, shall be grafted in: for God is able to graft them in again."[32]

"And you, Gentiles, be not high minded, but fear, for if God spared not the natural branches, neither will He spare thee."[33]

---

[26] Acts 17.29-30
[27] Jeremiah 31.31 (KJV)
[28] Jer. 31.31-33 (KJV)
[29] Rev.1.9
[30] Luke 17.20-21
[31] Romans 11.8-11 (Paraphrased)
[32] Ro. 11.23 (ASV)
[33] Ro. 11.20-21 (ASV)

PART I
ON A ROAD
LEADING TO ROME

The resurrected Jesus had told His disciples not to part from Jerusalem, but to wait for the promise of the Father for the outpouring of the Holy Spirit. "You shall receive power after the Holy Spirit is come upon you, and you shall be witnesses unto me, both in Jerusalem, and in all Judea, and in Samaria, and unto the utmost part of the earth."

That meant that His disciples would be preaching and teaching, not to the Jews only, but also the Greeks, and it meant that from the day of Pentecost, they would be carrying the message to the North, to the South, to the East, and to the West.

PENTECOST

In the ninth hour on the day of Pentecost, 40 days after the resurrection of Jesus, a great and mighty wind filled the house where they were sitting, and tongues of fire lashed all about them and they were all filled with the Holy Ghost. Devout Jews gathered from every nation under Heaven and they were amazed that every man could hear what was being said in his native tongue. Some said they were all full of wine, but they all wondered what it meant.

PETER ADDRESSES THE MULTITUDE

Then Peter, who was in the multitude, spoke up to say that no one was drunk. It was only the third hour of the day, and he said, "This is the day spoken of by the prophet Joel;[34]

> 'and it shall come to pass in the last days, I will pour out of my Spirit upon all flesh: and your sons and your daughters shall prophesy, and your young men shall see visions, and your old men shall dream dreams:...and I will show wonders in heaven, above, and signs on the earth beneath... and it shall come to pass that whosoever shall call on the name of the Lord shall be saved.'"

"You men of Israel, you very well know that Jesus Christ was a man approved and sent by God, for you have seen the signs and wonders and the mighty works that God did through Him, works that no man can do except God be with him, but you delivered Him to the wicked hands of heathen men to be crucified." This same Jesus has God raised up, setting Him free from the pangs of death, and has made Him both Lord and Christ.

When the multitude heard these things, they asked, "What, then, shall we do?" Peter answered, "Repent and be baptized for the remission of sin...and you shall receive the power of the Holy Ghost, for the promise is unto you and your children... and to as many as the Lord, our God, shall call. Then they that received His Word were baptized, and about three thousand souls were added to their number."

---

[34]Acts 2.16-21 (KJV)

STEPHEN

With more than five thousand believers now in the city of Jerusalem, some widows were being overlooked in the daily distribution of the charities. The apostles, therefore, called the multitude of disciples together and asked them to choose seven men to take over the work of "serving tables," "and we will give ourselves to prayer and to the ministry of the word."

The Bible does not tell us anything of the work of the other five men that were selected, but Stephen and Philip, under the direction of God's Spirit, proved to be proficient, both in the distribution of goods to the needy and in the preaching of the Word as well.

Stephen, full of grace and power wrought great "signs and wonders" among the people," but he was hailed before the Sanhedrin on charges of blasphemy. Jewish zealots hired men to accuse Stephen of blasphemy and to testify falsely that he unceasingly proclaims that Jesus of Nazareth will destroy the temple and change the customs of Moses. The high priest, then, turned to Stephen and asked him, "Are these things so?"

Stephen began, immediately, to show that his accusers were just like their forefathers, who over and over, according to their own history, provoked God by their disobedience, and God had consistently responded, on the basis of their unwillingness to hear him and change their ways as a "stubborn and stiff-necked people."[35] He testified that Jesus, indeed, spoke of the destruction of the temple, not as portrayed by the false witnesses,[36] but in reference to His own crucifixion and

---

[35] See Exodus32.9 & 33.3-5; Deuteronomy 9.6-13; 2Chronicles 30.8; Leviticus 26.41; Jeremiah 6.10 & 9.26 & Ezekiel 44.7,9

[36] Mark 14.58,

resurrection. What He said was "Destroy this temple, and in three days I will raise it up." [37]

Stephen, then delivered the final blow of his message, and he said, "You uncircumcised in heart and ears, you do always resist the Holy Ghost and neither hear, nor understand what God would have you do."[38]
They were cut to the heart, and they gnashed on him with their teeth, but he, being filled with the Holy Spirit, cried out, "Behold, I see the heavens opened and the Son of Man standing on the right hand of God."

They stopped their ears, and rushed upon him, and threw him out of the city. There they stoned him as he kneeled down and cried out in a loud voice, "Lord, lay not this sin to their charge.

Saul stood by, as he later testified, "...when the blood of Stephen, thy witness was shed, I, also was standing by and approving, and keeping the garments of those who killed him."[39]

Saul proceeded to ravish the church, entering their houses, dragging off men and women and committing them to prison. The persecution was thorough and unrelenting, but those who were scattered abroad went everywhere spreading the good news.[40]

THE SCATTERED DISCIPLES

PHILLIP

Shortly after the outbreak of the persecution and the scattering of the people, Philip first went to the city of Samaria to proclaim the gospel, and then he went to the

---

[37] John 2.19,20 (KJV)
[38] Jer.4.4 Similar use of the word circumcision
[39] Luke 22.20
[40] Acts 8. 2-4, *The Century Bible, The Acts, pp.208-209*

South, from Jerusalem into Gaza. There, he met an official of Candace, the Queen of Ethiopia, who had gone to Jerusalem to worship, and was on his way home. He was sitting in his chariot reading from the prophet Isaiah and asked Philip to explain it to him. Philip began at that point to teach unto him Jesus and to explain how the death of Christ and other events of days, just past, had been foretold.[41,42].

As they continued on the way, the man said, "Behold, here is water; what hinders me from being baptized? Then he stopped the chariot, and Philip baptized him. When they came up out of the water, the Spirit caught away Philip, and the man saw him no more, but he went on his way rejoicing.

THE APOSTLE PETER

Other than for a few episodes in Peter's life, which Luke presents to us,[43] The Acts of the Apostles is devoted almost exclusively to the labors of Saul. The other apostles are scarcely mentioned. Especially important, however, for all people, for all time, is the vision that Peter saw, and the encounter that he had with Cornelius the centurion. He learned that no one should be called "common or unclean."

Christianity would not be just another tribal religion for those of the circumcision, but a universal calling for all people and the pathway to Truth for all time.

Some members of the church of Jerusalem contended with Peter for entering the home of uncircumcised men, which was conduct against the Jewish law. Peter, then, told them the story of his visit with Cornelius.

---

[41] Acts 8.26-39, *The Century Bible*
[42] Isaiah 53
[43] Acts 9.32-12.19

SAUL OF TARSUS

Without doubt, Stephen's eloquent discourse infuriated Saul, for after his violent persecution of the Christians in Jerusalem, he went to the high priest for letters of approval to search out and arrest any Christians that may be found in Damascus. He had heard of the growing number in that city, and he believed he would be doing God a service by exterminating the religion of Christ.

He would continue his persecution, and he would bind the destroyers of the Law of Moses and bring them back to Jerusalem, for he had no doubt that the continued presence of the sect in Damascus would result in the subversion of the law, the preservation of which he considered of supreme importance.

Before Saul could get to Damascus, however, a blinding light struck him, and he heard a voice call out, saying, Saul, Saul, why do you persecute me? I am Jesus of Nazareth, the one you are persecuting." The voice from the Lord God and the blinding light were so spectacular that Saul was transformed almost immediately from a persecutor into a believer, and he was given instructions to go on to Damascus and meet with Ananias, through whom he would receive his sight and be filled with the Holy Ghost.

From that time forward, Saul was a marked man. He began to preach Christ in the synagogues, but the Jews sought to kill him. He went to Arabia where he spent three years before returning to his home in Tarsus.

PAUL, THE APOSTLE

Saul received a dramatically life-changing call for the special work that God had for him to do among the

Gentles. (He was Saul among the Hebrews and Paul to the Greeks). He thought of himself as a Hebrew of the Hebrews, having received his education at the feet of Gamaliel. That and the fact that his mother was a Gentile meant that he could learn and understand the lesson, more thoroughly than Peter, that no one should be called "common or unclean."

Barnabas sought out Paul and brought him to Antioch. There, they labored a year together and "taught many people." For every congregation they gathered, they appointed elders, and with prayer and fasting, they commended them to the Lord, on whom they had believed. Antioch became a great Christian center, of equal importance to that of Jerusalem.

THE FIRST MISSIONARY JOURNEY

As Barnabas and Paul ministered among the people of Antioch, God called them out to work "in the regions beyond," and they departed on what we now call Paul's first missionary journey.

Paul and Barnabas sailed from Cyprus to Perga, in Pamphilia. From there, they journeyed to Antioch in Pisidia and visited the synagogue, and on the invitation of the rulers of the synagogue Paul preached with such effect that the next Sabbath almost the entire city came to hear him.

The gathering of the multitudes aroused the animosity of the Jews, which led the missionaries to turn their attention to focus on the Gentiles, who gave glory to God that the gospel was for them also. Then, Paul and Barnabas moved on, with similar results in the cities of Lycaonia, Lystra, and Derbe.

At Lystra, the people wanted to worship Paul and Barnabas for healing a cripple, but hostile Jews from

Antioch and Iconium raised a mob and they took Paul and stoned him. They made their return trip through the same cities, "confirming the souls of the disciples, exhorting them to continue in their faith" with warnings of the tribulations that awaited them, "and when they had appointed for them elders in every church and had prayed with fasting, they commended them unto the Lord, on whom they had believed."

THE JERUSALEM CONFERENCE

When Paul and Barnabas were back in Antioch of Syria, "certain men came down from Judea and taught the brethren, saying, except ye be circumcised after the custom of Moses, ye cannot be saved." This caused such a disturbance in the church that it was determined that Paul and Barnabas and certain others should go to Jerusalem to talk to the apostles and elders about the question. As they were on their way and passing through Phoenicia and Samaria, they declared the joyful tidings of the conversion of the Gentiles.

When they arrived in Jerusalem, they were received by the apostles and elders and "rehearsed all things that God had dome with them." Some of the Pharisees who believed insisted that these Gentile converts must be circumcised and charged to keep the law of Moses, but Peter spoke up to rehearse his experience with the conversion of the gentiles and the many who had already received the Holy Ghost, without distinction, between them and the Jews of the circumcision.

After Paul and Barnabas gave an account of the signs and wonders that God had carried out through them, James, who seemed to be the most Judaizing of all the apostles, expressed his judgment "that we trouble them not which turn to God from the Gentiles ..., but ask them to "abstain from things sacrificed to idols, and from blood, and from things strangled, and from fornication; from which if ye keep yourselves, it shall be well with you."[44]

With the approval of the whole church, two men, Judas and Silas where chosen from their number to accompany Paul and Barnabas back to Antioch with a letter to rebuke those who had troubled the Antiochian brethren. Judas and Silas would emphasize the decision of the brethren and present the matters mentioned by James and it brought about what was thought to be a good understanding between these two primitive churches.

THE SECOND MISSIONARY JOURNEY

Paul, about A.D. 46 or 47, suggested to Barnabas that they revisit the new Christian brethren in the cities where they had preached, but they disagreed on the question of taking Mark. Therefore, Barnabas took Mark with himself and sailed away to Cyprus.

Paul took Silas "and went through Syria and Cilicia confirming the churches," then they came to Derbe and Lystra where Timothy was born. Being one of Paul's most devoted followers, he made plans to have him come with them. Paul took Timothy and circumcised him "because of the Jews which were in those quarters," apparently meaning that it was in deference to the Jews that were in the area.[45] The fact that Timothy's mother was a Jew may have had something to do with that decision as well.

When they left the area of Derbe and Lystra, they had planned to go into Bithynia, but the Holy Spirit led

---

[44] Acts 15.29
[45] The Century Bible, Acts 16.1-5

them the other way, and they went down to Troas. During the night a vision of a man from Macedonia appeared to Paul. He was standing, beseeching him, "come over to Macedonia and help us."

Paul interpreted this as God's call to service. They set sail from Troas to Samothrace and Neapolis, and made their way to Philippi, and the door was opened for the preaching of the Gospel to the Western World. Philippi was the first Macedonian city to be evangelized. Lydia, a seller of purple, and all her household were converted, and Paul and his company were given shelter in her home.

As they were going to their place of worship, Paul cast out an evil spirit from a slave girl "having a spirit of divination," who brought her masters much gain, which led to the imprisonment and beating of Paul and Silas.

About midnight Paul and Silas were singing hymns and suddenly there was a great earthquake. The foundations of the prison-house were shaken. Their bonds were loosed and the prison doors were opened. The jailer was awakened from sleep, and seeing the prison doors opened, he drew his sword and was about to kill himself, but Paul cried with a loud voice, saying, "Do thyself no harm for we are all here."

The jailor trembled and fell down at the feet of Paul and Silas, and said, "Sirs, what must I do to be saved?" And he said, "Believe on the Lord Jesus, and thou shalt be saved, thou and thy house." It not yet dawn, but the Jailor washed the stripes of Paul and Silas who then took him and all his family through the baptismal waters.

When it was day, Paul and Silas were back in prison and the Jailor guarding them. The magistrates sent word by the sergeants to let Paul and Silas go, but Paul reported that they as Roman citizens had been beaten publicly, and they would not leave privately. When the magistrates heard these words, they, indeed feared the consequences from higher authorities and came to the jail and personally brought them out.

After going by the house of Lydia and seeing and comforting the brethren, they made their way to Thessalonica, where he commended their "work of faith and labor of love and patience of hope," but they were soon driven from the city by Jewish opposition.

In Berea, the Jews received the Word with all readiness of mind, examining the Scriptures daily whether these things were so."[46] Paul went on to Athens and left Silas and Timothy to carry on the work as Jews from Thessalonica arrived to arouse opposition to their labor.

Paul found the City of Athens full of idols, and curious and contemptuous listeners in abundance, but few were prepared to accept the truth, however, a few did.[47] When he saw an inscription that read, "TO THE UNKNOWN GOD," he preached a sermon and began by saying, "Him I declare unto you."

In Corinth, probably the most important city in Greece at the time, Paul performed some of his most fruitful labors over a longer period of time. He abode with fellow tentmakers Aquila and Priscilla and carried on a very successful work for about 18 months. Crispus, the ruler of the synagogue and all his family were believers, but there was so much opposition from the Jews, he held his meetings in the house of another convert.

The Jews, in the end, rose up against him and arraigned him before the judgment seat of Gallio, the proconsul, who refused to pronounce judgment against him, but Paul soon "sailed for Syria" and took Aquila and Priscilla with him.

---

[46] Acts 17.11 (ASV)
[47] One who believed was Dionysius, whom later tradition represented as the first to evangelize France. (A.H.N.)

They landed at Ephesus and Paul reasoned with the Jews in the synagogue. He declined an invitation to stay longer and sailed for Caesaria. He went up to salute the church in Jerusalem, then went on to Antioch.

During Paul's absence, (being in Antioch) an Alexandrian Jew named Apollos came to Ephesus. He was a learned man and "mighty in the Scriptures," but he knew only of the baptism of John, the baptism of repentance. When Aquila and Priscilla heard him, they took him and expounded unto him the way of God more carefully."

PAUL'S THIRD MISSIONARY JOURNEY

After spending some time in Antioch, Paul departed for Ephesus, revisiting the churches in Galatia and Phrygia on the way. On reaching Ephesus, he found other disciples there who had only the knowledge of the baptism of John, and had no knowledge of the Holy Ghost. Paul instructed them, and they were baptized "into the name of the Lord Jesus," and when he had laid his hands upon them, the Holy Ghost came upon them and they spoke with tongues, and prophesied."[48]

Paul now entered upon a remarkably successful work. He preached three months in the synagogue, then withdrew because of Jewish opposition and taught daily in a lecture hall, called the School of Tyrannus. Here, he taught for two years, and all who dwelt in Asia heard the Word of the Lord, both Jews and Greeks. Sick people were healed, demons were cast out, and fear fell upon them all, and the name of the Lord Jesus was magnified

Paul was about to leave Ephesus and move on to Macedonia, when an outcry was raised against the Christians. It was a disturbance led by idol-makers,

---

[48] The Century Bible, Acts 19.1-6,

whose trade was seriously affected by the outpouring of the Word of God. Then, the angry idol-makers led the mob into the great amphitheater chanting, "Great is Diana of the Ephesians," and they continued to chant for the space of two hours.

Through skilful oratory, the town clerk was able to quiet them down by pointing out how foolish it would be to compromise the privileges of the city as keepers of the temple of the great goddess, Diana. That's what could happen, he told them, if they followed this path of destruction, when any damage done could be settled through normal procedures in a court of law.

Paul journeyed to Macedonia and to Greece, revisiting and exhorting the churches that he had previously founded. In Corinth, he spent three months. "No doubt much of his thought was devoted to the final stages of his great collection for the poor in the church at Jerusalem."[49] Returning through Macedonia he sailed from Philippi to Troas, where on the first day of the week, the brethren "were gathered together to break bread." Paul, intending to leave the next day, spoke until midnight and a young man, "borne down with deep sleep, fell from a window of the third floor."

It was Paul's hope to be in Jerusalem on the day of Pentecost. To hasten his journey, on their arrival at Miletus, he sent to Ephesus for the elders of the church to come to him. In his farewell charge he warned them that grievous wolves would enter in among them, not sparing the flock. He tenderly exhorted them to take heed unto themselves and to all the flock over which the Holy Ghost had made them bishops. As for himself, he expected bonds and imprisonment. They would see his face no more.

---

[49]The Century Bible, Acts 20.3-6

OTHER MINISTRIES

After Peter became involved in work outside the city of Jerusalem, James the brother of Jesus came to be recognized as the leader of the mother church. It does not appear that he ever abandoned the belief that all Jewish Christians are obliged to keep the ceremonial law, but he recognized Gentiles as converts without circumcision, but as a Jew, he felt bound to observe the whole law and to require other Jewish converts to do the same.

The information in the following paragraphs about James and some of the other apostles came to us through "early tradition," usually meaning historians not far removed from the time, which may not be verified, and which may come with contradictory information.

There is early tradition to the effect that sometime after Paul was sent to Rome, Annas, the high priest called the Sanhedrin together to secure the condemnation of James, because his confession led to the conversion of so many Jews. When he did, some leaders of the Jews took James and cast him from the pinnacle of the temple, then stoned him and beat him to death.

Jude, another brother of Jesus, and an apostle, wrote the short epistle under his name, and it is believed that he stayed in the ministry with the church in Jerusalem, although there is no Biblical evidence.

Early tradition represents the apostles Andrew, Matthew, and Bartholomew as laboring in the region of the Black Sea, and that Thomas, Thaddeus, and Simon the Canaanite, three other apostles, went to the remote East as far as India.

Mark is believed to have labored in Egypt, and that he founded the church in Alexandria. He was with Paul during his Roman imprisonment, and with Peter at the time when Peter wrote his first epistle.

We have no further information about Barnabas after he separated from Paul, except that he labored for a time on the Island of Cyprus and some early historians think that he wrote the Epistle to the Hebrews. Neither do we know anything more about Apollos, but Martin Luther thinks that he wrote the Epistle to the Hebrews.

Titus was closely associated with Paul in his missionary labors, was with Paul during part of his Roman Imprisonment, and served as missionary or pastor of the church of Ephesus for an extended period of time.

Luke, "the beloved physician" and author of the gospel by that name, and of the book of Acts, was closely associated with Paul on his missionary journeys and during his imprisonment in Rome.

Finally, John, the youngest of the apostles, the "One whom Jesus loved," was author of the Gospel under his name, and he wrote three epistles which are included in the New Testament. His first epistle stresses errors in the Christian doctrine of the time, particularly the belief that the Word became incarnate in appearance only. He lived and labored in the area of "the seven churches of Asia" long past the time of the other apostles, and worked under the trying conditions of persecution during the reigns of both Nero and Domitian. It was during the time of Domitian that John found it prudent to use apocalyptic form of writing in his communication with the churches.

The death of the apostles brought an end to the leadership of those who had walked with Christ and it brought an end of what we consider the Apostolic Age, the time referred to by the prophecy of Joel, "...and I will show wonders in heaven above, and signs in the earth beneath; blood, and fire, and vapor of smoke..."

LIFE AFTER THE APOSTLES

We are fortunate to have available two separate historical accounts that show the simplicity and dedication of the lives of early Christians and how the Spirit of Christ lived in them in their appointed fields of service at the close of the Apostolic Age, near A.D. 100.

Emperor Domitian, who was carrying out a severe persecution, is said to have heard that the relatives of Jesus still lived in Palestine and that he suspected them of political ambition. When they were brought before him and he saw that they were "poor rustics," he soon was convinced that the kingdom of Christ was truly a heavenly and spiritual kingdom and was not a threat to any earthly kingdom. He then let them go and by a decree put a stop to the persecution of the church.

The other account was about Christians just a few years later. Pliny, who was governor in the eastern province of Bithynia (in Asia Minor), in correspondence with Emperor Trajan, revealed that he had punished some of his subjects for being Christians in order to get them to return to the neglected (pagan) temples. To Pliny, Christianity was a bad superstition, but in describing the Christians, he said that it was their custom to assemble before light in the morning, sing a hymn to Christ, and promise one another not to commit any crime or evil deed. Later in the day, he said, they would have a meal together.

THE ROMAN RELIGION

The religion of the Romans was much like that of the Greeks, but the Romans practiced their religion with more dignity and order. Their gods represented the powers of nature that took on human-like personalities.

Every aspect of nature, including the sun and the moon, and the stars and the planets, was thought of as being a god, with the power to affect men for good or evil.

Religion was promoted and administered by the State to serve the interests of the State. It was not a matter of feeling, but always a matter of form and required the observance of all ceremonies and saying all prayers exactly as prescribed. The slightest mistake in word or gesture would ruin the entire proceeding. The same rite was often repeated many times because of slight defects in utterance or manipulation.

Theoretically, every householder was the priest of his own household, but the emphasis upon exactitude, along with the difficulty, made it seem necessary for experts to perform the ceremonies. This gave great power to the priests.

From the founding of the Republic, there was a college of pontiffs headed by a Pontifex Maximus, whose business it was to supervise all the religious affairs of the state. These pontiffs were experts in religious matters. They alone had perfect familiarity with the details of the rituals, the names and the functions of the many gods, and precisely what god it was necessary to appease in order to receive a favor.

In its early days, the Roman religion promoted virtue and honor, but as Rome conquered Greece and other territories to the east and enforced its law, Rome was gradually absorbing the culture and licentious living of the Greek.

When the republic was transformed into an empire in B.C. 31, Augustus strove in vain to check the process of decay and to restore the national religion to its pristine position. He assumed personally the office of Pontifex Maximus to become not only the head of the state, but also the head of religion as an institution of the

State. Emperors, no matter how corrupt and despicable, came to be worshipped as gods.

THE OUTLAWED RELIGION

From its first appearance, Christianity was generally considered to be a Jewish sect, but when considered separately, it was a secret society and contrary to the law of the Romans. Cicero expressed it this way:

> "Separately, let no one have gods, nor may they worship privately new or foreign gods unless they have been publicly recognized."

With the Romans, the State was the chief thing. Religion was to be promoted only in so far as it served the interests of the State. Idolatrous and immoral practices were intertwined into every phase of the social life of the pagans. Christians could not participate in these practices and so were looked upon as atheists and enemies of the human race.

The Christians could not be satisfied with the Roman notion that the highest priority of religion is to serve the interests of the state. Christianity sought to be universal and win all humankind to their cause. For that reason they could be accused of being dangerous or even an enemy of the state.

Christians were known to assemble at night, secretly, and in considerable numbers. What could be the reason, but the gratification of lust? It became easy to believe the worst of those who also spoke of partaking of the body and the blood of the one they worshipped.

There was a total misunderstanding by the masses of people. Christians everywhere were persecuted as a result of this popular hatred, and it was the most upright rulers, those who made the most vigorous efforts to uphold the Roman law, that made Christianity illegal.

FALSE TEACHERS ABOUND

The early Christians had the teachings of Christ and the apostles, but there were also many false teachers. Christianity drew its converts from Judaism and paganism, and could not long avoid absorbing, to some extent, their ways of thinking. There were soon Jewish and pagan types of Christianity.

THE JUDAIZERS

The Jewish Christians, who resented from the very first, the preaching of Paul and Barnabas to the Gentiles, said that you can't be a Christian without being a Jew first. You have to be circumcised, and you have to perform all of the ceremonies, and obey all of the requirements of the ceremonial law according to tradition.

Peter, Paul and Barnabas had won the day for the Gentiles at the Jerusalem Conference, some Judaizers continued to dog the steps of the missionaries until Christianity came to be recognized as a separate religion.

THE GNOSTICS

Among other false teachers were the Gnostics, a pagan philosophical system whose adherents were fond of the *Mysteries*, the elaborate and pompous ceremonies drawn from Greek and Egyptian secret rites. They believed that the Supreme Being could not create an imperfect world; therefore, they rejected most of the Bible. They considered morality to be far less important than solving such *mysteries*. Some Gnostics were utterly without moral scruples, saying it doesn't matter what the flesh does, it is the spirit that counts. Others practiced the most rigid asceticism (or self-denial and self- mortification).

Professing, as did the Gnostics, to have all the answers to the problems of the universe, and commending themselves to pious Christians by great earnestness and zeal, and usually by ascetic living, they easily gained followers, despite all efforts of the teachers of sound doctrine.

Gnostics, eventually, were identified and excluded from the churches, but their influence led the way in mixing pagan life and thought into the Christianity that would prevail in the third and following centuries.

TELLING THE STORY

The story of Christianity after New Testament times is told by a series of Christian writers, most of whom were pastors or respected leaders. Some have called them the "Early Fathers." They recorded not only times of heroic living and dying, but also times of increasing corruption in the church.

Because of the way they were misunderstood by others, the need for Christians to explain (or justify) their faith pressed upon them, but at first most of their writings were simple expressions of faith. They showed no knowledge of pagan philosophy, and they seemed too much occupied with the interests of their own religion to enter into the business of disproving false beliefs.

IGNATIUS AND POLYCARP

Two of these early writers were Ignatius and Polycarp. Both died for their Christian faith. Ignatius was pastor of the church at Antioch. It is said that he wrote his epistles while being transported to Rome, where he was executed early in the second century. He frequently exhorted Christians to obey their pastors, or bishops, and to look to such men as being in the place of Christ.

In the centuries to come, church leaders who strove for power and authority interpreted the admonition to obey in a very literal sense. By misrepresenting his works and producing false documents in his name to support their own ideas, they laid the chief groundwork for the development of a ruling hierarchy.

We know of Polycarp through Irenaeus, a later writer. Irenaeus said that he knew Polycarp as a disciple of the Apostle John. He distinctly remembers how Polycarp used to describe the times he was with John and the others who had been with the Lord, how he learned from the apostles, and how he lovingly treasured up in his memory and frequently talked to others about the things that he had learned.

Irenaeus mentions a beautiful account of the martyrdom of Polycarp, about A.D. 155, which was probably written by the members of the church of Smyrna where Polycarp was pastor for many years.

JUSTIN MARTYR

Justin Martyr represents the next generation of writers. They felt that patient endurance might be carried to an extreme – that it was better to live and labor than to suffer martyrdom. They tried to justify the Christian faith and wrote the most important of their works to emperors to secure for Christians the right to exist.

We know from the writings of Justin Martyr that he was a Samaritan and saw in his youth a good deal of persecution of Christians, and admired their endurance. We could call him the original Pilgrim, for like Pilgrim of *Pilgrim's Progress;* he searched long and hard to find rest for his troubled soul.

He studied for a while with a stoic, but finding himself none the wiser with regard to God, he went to a peripatetic (in the tradition of Aristotle), who "was a sharp fellow in his own eyes."

Soon disgusted with him, he betook himself to a celebrated Pythagorean who insisted that he must learn music, astronomy, and geometry as necessary preparation for philosophical studies. Greatly troubled on account of this rebuff, he went to an intelligent Platonist, from whom he learned the Platonic philosophy.

For a time, he was highly elated with his progress, but while walking near the seashore, he fell in with an aged Christian with whom he conversed freely, and by whom he learned and believed the way of truth.

We know very little about Justin's life after his conversion, except that he continued to wear his philosopher's robe and went about seeking to win men to the Gospel. He frequently sought conferences with men of education and met violent opposition from the philosophers about the court of Emperor Marcus Arelius. He met his martyrdom about the year 165, probably due to their animosity.

Justin's first *Apology* (or justification of Christianity) was to show that Christians are not criminals, and the fact that they prefer death proves they are innocent. He argues that they should not be condemned without a fair hearing; that they should not be blamed for refusing to worship images (an absurdity); nor for believing that the creator of all things "does not desire gifts." The latter refers to the Pagan practice of offering of gifts in striving to appease their gods.

DEFINING THE FAITH

A number of highly educated scholars grew up under a greatly improved Christian culture in the middle of the second century. They began to express themselves more carefully and more fully on the wild speculations of the Gnostics with regard to such matters as the nature of God, the origin of the world, the origin of sin, the divinity of the Son of God, His incarnation, and the nature of the Holy Spirit.

They began to study the gospels and the writings of the apostles more carefully and to more completely define Christian doctrine to distinguish it from non-Christian heresy, thus setting forth the idea of an orthodox universal church.

For the first time, the writings which in a century or two would form the New Testament, were quoted as Scripture equal in authority to the Old Testament. Irenaeus, a disciple of Polycarp, was a student of the Greek classics and both the Old and the New Testaments. He was acquainted with the false teachings of the day, but above all, he was a man of great faith and dedication. When the pastor of the church at Lyons suffered martyrdom, he bravely took the dangerous position.

As one of the most diligent and knowledgeable students of the Christian literature of his time, Irenaeus insisted that when the Scriptures are plain and unambiguous, they should not be explained ambiguously according to the fancy of the interpreter, and ambiguous passages should not be made a source of doctrine.

Among the things that he wrote was probably the first Christian declaration of faith, and he wrote five books against heresies, about A.D. 185, toward the close of his busy life.

IRENAEUS

A formalizing tendency and centralization of authority had already begun at Rome and in Asia Minor. Life and worship were becoming more strictly controlled than ever before. Irenaeus believed the church should be a unified organization, but liberty and independence, to him, were fundamental principles, and he did not agree with the growing centralization of authority.

By this time the church at Rome had great prestige. Its position in a great city, its administrative ability, and its readiness to send contributions to needy Christians in other places caused it to be looked up to and to be frequently appealed to in matters of controversy. Irenaeus believed that the church at Rome was established by Peter and Paul, who appointed successors, and this belief added great weight to its prestige.

Victor, chief pastor at Rome from about 189-199, had been arrogant enough to break off communion with churches who disagreed with him on the date for celebrating Easter. Irenaeus rebuked Victor severely, clearly indicating that he did not accept the superiority of the bishop of Rome over all other bishops, saying:

> "Christ's apostles have ordained that no one shall disturb men's consciences with regard to such things. It is not right to tear asunder the

bonds of Christian communion on account of festivals and seasons, knowing as we do from the prophets that such things celebrated in hatred and discord do not please God."

VICTOR, BISHOP OF ROME AND HIS SUCCESSORS

Victor was a very stern man, and many had been restless under his rigorous discipline. In 199 he was succeeded by Zephyrinus, a man of little moral or intellectual weight, who permitted the flock to be led astray by all sorts of false teachers; and under the influence of one Callistus, permitted various moral delinquencies in the church.

Callistus, a slave, had been entrusted with a large sum of money. He had embezzled it, was imprisoned, and then released. After his release, he caused a riot in a Jewish synagogue, for which he was banished to the mines of Sardinia. Having escaped from the mines through the help of Marcia, the emperor's favorite concubine, he returned to Rome a freed man. He became the right hand man to Zephyrinus, and then succeeded him as chief pastor in the year 219.

The emperors in power from 180-249 were cruel and vindictive, yet their policies were mostly favorable toward Christianity, and Christians were generally immune from persecution. It was during such times that the numbers of Christians multiplied, and many were brought into the Church who were little changed from their pagan ways, and morality in the churches declined.

Marcia, who may have been responsible for the lenient attitude of Commodus (emperor from 180 to 193) toward Christians, took Christians under her protection. She secured the deliverance of many from the mines and sought in many ways to further their interests. Whether Marcia was a member of the Roman church is uncertain, but considering the circumstances at that time, as described by Hippolytus, it was very possible she was a member of the church.

HIPPOLYTUS

Hippolytus was active in the church at Rome during the pastorates of Zephyrinus and Callistus. It is said that he was a disciple of Irenaeus, and he ranked with Tertullian, Clement of Alexandria, and Origen as one of the greatest scholars and theologians of the age.

He was a voluminous writer of many treatises. One of these was discovered in 1842 in the monastery on Mt. Athos. The most remarkable part of the document, the "Refutation of all Heresies," is Book IX, in which the heresy of Noetus (discussed under Gnostic Heresies) is denounced as the cause of the moral laxity and doctrinal unsoundness of Callistus, who became chief pastor of the church at Rome in 219.

There were in the church at Rome at that time two distinct parties, one rigorous in discipline, led by Hippolytus, and a larger party that placed much less emphasis on moral standards, represented by Callistus and supported by the wealthy classes. Most of those in the latter party had become members only when it was safe to do so, when there was no threat of persecution.

TERTULLIAN

Tertullian, another great Christian writer, was born about A.D. 150 to 160. He was a "rugged and eccentric genius."[50] Originally a lawyer, he was converted to

---

[50]Schaff,Vol.II,p16.

Christianity in mature life and served as a presbyter (pastor or elder) in Africa until about 220.

By way of reaction against the lax discipline and scandalous behavior, particularly as existed in the church at Rome under Zephyrinus, he was carried away by the rigor and enthusiasm of the Montanists, who offered the most decided opposition to the heresy of Noetus.

The Montanists claimed to be especially instructed by the Spirit in visions toward self-denial and rigorous discipline, making religion largely a matter of outward observances. They exalted virginity, widowhood, and martyrdom, and claimed to have special revelations through visions that second marriages were equivalent to adultery.

Tertullian wrote in glowing terms of the magical effects of water baptism, but he believed that sins committed after baptism were unpardonable, therefore, he thought that no one should be baptized until ready to guard his life most scrupulously. (See Gnostics Heresies)

Tertullian did not agree with the trend of the time of holding authority and tradition above "truth;" he was one of the "strongest champions of orthodoxy over Gnostic heresies,"[51] but because of his widespread authority many of his Montanistic views infiltrated into the mainstream thinking of the church.

As worldliness and corruption in the churches increased, the rigorous stance of the Montanists increased, until they and like-minded groups separated themselves from the churches and sought lives of self-denial in monasteries or in the caves of the mountains.

---

[51] Schaff, Vol.II, pp.16, 17.

ORIGEN

Origen "was the greatest divine [or theologian] and one of the noblest characters of his age, equally distinguished for genius, learning, industry, and enthusiasm for the knowledge of truth."[52]

Born about A.D. 185 of Christian parents, he could repeat from memory large parts of the Scriptures, and often perplexed his intelligent father by the subtlety of his questions. His father, Leonides, suffered martyrdom about the year 202 as Origen encouraged him to steadfastness as he, himself, was being restrained from giving himself up for martyrdom.

From childhood, throughout life, he practiced a rigorous asceticism. He possessed but one coat, and no shoes. He rarely ate meat, never drank wine, devoted much of the night to study and prayer, and slept on the bare floor. He apparently made himself a eunuch, believing that Christ advocated such action in His words recorded by Matthew, "...and there be eunuchs which have made themselves eunuchs for the Kingdom of Heaven's sake."[53]

He was appointed catechist at Alexandria at the age of 18 years, and held that post for about 25 years. The remainder of his life was spent at Caesarea, in Palestine, where he conducted a theological school.

He was the first to use scientific and critical methods to study and analyze the bible, and there is no writer of the early church to whom we are so indebted for biblical interpretation. He was one of the most voluminous of writers and produced systematic expressions of Christian doctrine, practical works, such as on prayer and

---

[52] Schaff, Vol. II, pp. 21-22.
[53] Matt 19.12.

martyrdom, and answered scurrilous works against Christianity written by pagans.

It was Origen's teaching that the Son was "begotten by the Father," yet was "eternal," more than any other of his doctrines, that played such an important part in settling the issue on the divinity of Christ.

Origen believed that questions not answered specifically by Scripture should be answered, as far as possible, in conformity with Scripture, but allowed each person much freedom in such matters.

Accordingly, in one of his great works, he clearly set out the articles of faith of the universal church and then proceeded to give his opinion on other questions not clearly answered by Scripture. These speculations caused great controversies for centuries.

CYPRIAN PROMOTES CENTRALIZATION OF POWER

Up to the time of Irenaeus, the distinction between presbyters and bishops, if any, was by no means clear, but by the time of Cyprian (200-258), who became bishop of the Carthaginian church at a very young age, many churches had become large bodies with several presbyters (or pastors).

As the distribution of alms and other responsibilities assumed vast proportions, it was necessary to have someone to oversee the work. The one who was chosen for that position became known as bishop. This, in effect, made him chairman of the board of presbyters and the administrator of discipline.

Disputes would frequently arise which would require action by the bishop. Because of such occasions, the strong feeling arose, and seemed to be justified, that the bishop should be given greater authority in order to preserve unity.

Bishops, when they had strong governing talent, and were popular, gradually gained the upper hand. That's what happened in Cyprian's case. He asserted the divine right of bishops, as successors of the apostles, to have supremacy over presbyters, perhaps not considering that one day he may have to submit to a decision against himself by a higher authority.

Having a person with the power to settle arguments undoubtedly had some effect in promoting tranquility and order for a time, but the same tendency that led to centralization of power in the bishop led to the centralization of power in the head of the Universal Church, and rule by the priesthood in years to come.

The general tendency of the Church from that time forward was toward form and ceremony, with greater authority being placed into the hands of Church officials. The idea of the spiritual unity of the church, which was advocated by Irenaeus, was easily transformed into that of outward unity.

CYPRIAN AND THE PERSECUTIONS OF 250 TO 260

The thousandth birthday of the city of Rome was being celebrated when Decius Trajan returned from the Gothic War as the new emperor. It was obviously determined that only by exterminating Christianity and restoring the pagan state religion could unity and stability of the empire be achieved, for in A.D. 250 Decius issued the first imperial edict aimed at the universal suppression of Christianity, and Cyprian went into retirement.

Christians, everywhere, were required to conform to the state religion by participating in its ceremonies and appear before the magistrates to offer sacrifices to the gods. Flight was not hindered, but fugitives' property was confiscated, and the penalty was death for those who returned. Those who refused to offer sacrifices to the gods were threatened, then subjected to repeated tortures, hunger and thirst, with special severity employed toward pastors and bishops.

Immunity from persecution during good times brought many into the churches who had no idea of the meaning of true Christianity, and lamentable worldliness overcame many of the clergy. It was mainly of these that Cyprian wrote,

> "Before the battle, many were conquered; without having met the enemy, many were cut down...."

On the other hand, there were great numbers who would neither flee nor sacrifice to pagan gods. They suffered the most terrible tortures; they were then either left to die in prison, or were at last cruelly executed.

THE CHURCH FACES PAGANIZATION AND CORRUPTION

From the year 260 to the time of Diocletian (284), the Christians suffered almost no persecution. They grew in number, wealth, church organization, and in worldliness. Pagans flowed into the churches, taking with them many of their habits of life and thought, as had happened in other periods of time when it was popular to do so.

As in paganism, Christian worship became a matter of form. As early as the middle of the second century the Lord's Prayer came to be generally used as a ritual. Gradually, other forms of prayer and praise were added until somewhat elaborate ceremonies had been introduced with full directions for worship and the administration of the ordinances.

External performance of ceremonies became more important than morality, and pompous ceremonies came to be used as a means both to satisfy deity and to maintain the respect and admiration of the people.

As pagans had been accustomed to worshipping a host of gods and goddesses, they selected the most honored Christian personalities to become the worshipped "saints." These were of course, Mary, the mother of Jesus, the apostles, and noted martyrs.

Christian charity was perverted to the notion that simply giving donations or practicing some kind of self-denial would secure the forgiveness of sins. A belief developed in the spiritual potency of baptismal waters, burial sites, places of worship, and the bones and relics of saints and martyrs. Such objects came to be considered "holy" and to have magical powers from which spiritual benefits would flow.

As is the case with all pagan religions, the ordinances came to be administered by a properly qualified priest, through whom, alone, the ordinary person could reap spiritual benefits.

By the time of the persecutions under Diocletian and his son-in-law, Galerius (284-305), the church was corrupt and worldly as never before. As in the Decian persecution, many hastened to deny the faith and to surrender their copies of the Scriptures, and many bore the most horrible tortures, who refused with their last breath to deny their faith.

THE RISE OF CONSTANTINE

Constantine succeeded his father as ruler in Britain and Gaul in the northwestern reaches of the Roman Empire. He was favorably disposed toward Christianity and protected Christians as his father had done during the persecutions.

Maxentius, the cruel and greedy ruler at Rome, provoked Constantine by openly planning a campaign to gain control of the entire West. After careful consideration, Constantine decided to face the tyrant and led his own forces in the direction of Rome. Success, he felt, would eventually make him head of the empire, but defeat, of course, would be utterly disastrous.

Aware that Maxentius had already called upon all the pagan gods, Constantine felt compelled to look for divine assistance elsewhere. He, therefore, made up his mind to invoke the aid of the God of the Christians, knowing of their aggressiveness and rapid growth. His troops had to be inspired. He declared that he had seen in the sky a banner in the form of a cross. He had one made like the one he claimed to have seen, and under this banner his army won a "glorious victory."

Soon after the victory, he had a statue of himself erected in Rome with a cross in his right hand. In his left hand, he held an inscription which gave credit to the cross for the liberation of the city from the yoke of tyranny.

In 313, the Edict of Milan was issued jointly by Constantine and Licinius, the emperor of the eastern provinces. It proclaimed liberty of conscience, the first known in history among civil governments, but Licinius, in 319 reversed the proclamation in his part of the empire and began a severe persecution of Christians. Constantine then conquered Licinius and became emperor of all the provinces, both in the East and in the West in 323.

CONSTANTINE AS HEAD OF THE CHURCH

As the Roman emperor was Pontifex Maximus of the pagan state religion, he would conveniently be honored with the same title when Christianity became the favored religion. In 324, Constantine is said to have promised every convert to Christianity twenty pieces of gold and a white baptismal robe. Twelve thousand men, with women and children in proportion, are said to have been baptized in Rome in one year.

Constantine's greatest concern seems to have been unity. He was almost indifferent toward doctrinal differences. Anxious to settle a dispute in the interest of peace, he convened the First General Council of the Universal Church, the Council of Nicea, and presided over it.

THE OFFICIAL RELIGION

Constantine favored Christianity and made it legal, but it was left by Theodosius, a half-century later, to make it the official and exclusive religion of the state. It brought an end to persecution and death for the Christians for their faith, and it ended the gladiatorial shows for all time, but when the empire smiled on Christianity, there were evil effects to be suffered.

When a law placed into effect the observance of the first day of the week as the Resurrection Day of the Lord, it became a legal festival. When temporal inducements were offered to Pagans for professing Christianity, multitudes of unchanged Pagans were brought into the churches and the churches assumed the magnificence of heathen temples. In imitating the pomp, the Christians would imitate the practices of Paganism, most of the members being brought up as Pagans, and were Christian in name only.

As pagans had been accustomed to worshipping a host of gods and goddesses in the form of images, they soon filled the churches with images of the most honored personalities of Christianity, which were, of course, Mary, the mother of Jesus, the apostles, and noted martyrs.

Bones and other relics of saints and martyrs; the cross, and the sign of the cross; the sepulcher of Christ; and other objects were said to be holy, and to have magical effects. Without the spiritual potency of baptismal waters, it was said, there is no means of salvation

Common to all pagan religions, the priest became the mediator between God and man, and the channel through which, alone, a person can receive spiritual benefits. Following priestly directions, which centered on the performance of rituals, was more important than morality. Ritualism and pompous ceremonies were thought to please God, and were used by the priests to secure and maintain the reverence of the people.

Hierarchical development was stimulated and bishops gained authority over presbyters. Church government was made a part of civil government, and as Rome was the seat of government in the West, the Nicene Council gave the Bishop of Rome authority over all the bishops in the West and that decree was enforced by the emperor, for in 31 B.C. as an effort to restore the national religion its former "pristine position," Augustine assumed, personally the office of Pontifex Maximus, thus combining in his own person civil and religious headship and his authority over the Church as an institution of the state.

There was widespread belief that outside the church there is no salvation, therefore persecution could be justified on the basis that some heretics could be brought back into the church (whether by choice, was a minor consideration). If some were slain, they were only made to meet their inevitable (and miserable) fate a little sooner. It was a question of saving some by eliminating corrupting influences, or letting them all go to perdition together.

The Lord's injunction, "compel them to come in" was interpreted literally and was used as authority for the use of force. Heresy came to be looked upon as the greatest possible evil, and the heretic was the worst enemy of God and man, and worthy of no humane consideration. Even Ambrose and Augustine, two of the greatest and most renowned bishops of the early centuries were in favor of forcible suppression of paganism and heresy. Many bishops led their people on violent onslaughts of pagan sanctuaries and hesitated not to shed blood to accomplish their purpose.

PART II
THROUGH THE LONG, DARK NIGHT

CENTERS OF POWER

Constantine considered religion to be a unifying force in the empire and upheld Christianity for that purpose, but the great majority of the Romans clung tenaciously to their old religion. This caused a division of loyalties that to him was a serious matter. Therefore, after defeating Licinius in the East, which gave him authority over both the Eastern and Western divisions of the empire, he removed the center of government from Rome and established a new capital at Byzantium, naming it in honor of himself.

The Church was supported by the State and given status as a means of promoting civil order and unity. Controversy within the Church was a cause of great concern and became a reason for strong action. As emperor, Constantine assumed, personally, the office of Pontifex Maximus and gave full recognition to Christianity as an institution of the State. In order to settle one of the great controversies of the time, he called the first general council of the Church, the Council of Nicea, and presided over it. He occupied himself with the suppression of heresy and legislated freely for the Church.

The sixth canon (or decree) of the Nicene Council, over which Constantine presided, officially recognized the authority of the bishops of certain metropolitan churches, based on the customs of the time.

Rome was recognized as having authority over all the cities of the West, and Alexandria and Antioch, in the East, were recognized as having authority over all cities in their respective provinces. There is no hint of any authority being given to Rome over any churches in the East, in fact, both Alexandria and Antioch were given the same authority over all churches in their provinces and are mentioned quite as prominently as Rome. Translated from the Greek, the canon reads:

> "Let the ancient usages which exist in Egypt, and Libya, and Pentapolis, remain in force, to the effect that the bishop of Alexandria should have authority over all these, since this [the exercise of authority over the provincial churches of the West] is customary also for the bishop who is in Rome; and similarly, both as to Antioch and in the other provinces, let the churches have their privileges secured to them."

At a later time, a clause, "Rome has always held the primacy," was added spuriously (or falsely) into the canon in an attempt to add credibility to the doctrine of Roman superiority. This deceitful addition to the text was first used, as far as we know, by the representatives of Leo the Great at the council of Chalcedon in 451.

CONDITIONS FAVOR ROME

When Constantine moved his imperial capital to Byzantium and renamed the city after himself, the church there had no claim to apostolic foundation, a dignity that was generally thought to be required for the seat of a patriarch. There was, therefore, by a sort of legal fiction, a transfer of dignity from another location.

Unlike the circumstances at Rome, there was little opportunity for the Patriarch of Constantinople to develop independent power. The immediate presence of the emperor in the same city and the patriarch's dependence on Antioch and Alexandria for an educated ministry detracted from his prestige.

Conditions were much more favorable for the growth of power of the Bishop of Rome, who, without the imperial presence, assumed the title of Pontifex Maximus, or Pope, having authority over all the bishops in the West.

Without the presence of the emperor, there existed in Italy either a weak imperial authority or none at all until the barbarian invasions in the fifth century. It was then that the imperial power collapsed, and the barbarian kingdoms reigned in Italy and the western provinces.

The barbarians did not consider the Church a threat, therefore the Church's machinery was left in place to become, at times, the only bulwark against total anarchy. The prestige thereby gained added immensely to the importance of the office of the pope.

HERETICAL AND LEGALISTIC MOVEMENTS

The churches of the Eastern division of the empire (also called Oriental) had a history of great concern with exact definition and hairsplitting, which kept them embroiled in controversy. The Western churches, true to the spirit of the Romans, were more practical in their decisions, including the practicality of making decisions which seemed best for the Church, such as preserving and increasing ecclesiastical power. Those tendencies were reflected in the nature of the controversies, with the result that most of the controversies would originate in the East.

THE GNOSTIC HERESIES

The germs of Gnosticism doubtlessly existed in apostolic times. Paul spoke of knowledge as "puffing up" [suggesting an egotistical attitude]. Evidence of Gnostic opposition to Christianity is seen in the writings of John, and Irenaeus testified that the Gospel of John was written to oppose Gnosticism. Simon Magus, according to a narrative in Acts, represented himself as "the great power of God." As an arch-heretic, it is likely that he was a forerunner, if not the founder, of Gnosticism.

The basis of Gnosticism was influenced by the conception of *Absolute Being* taught by Plato and Pythagoras. It was theorized that the Supreme Being could not have created a sinful world.

The chief aim of Gnosticism, therefore, was to account for the creation of a sinful and imperfect world without compromising the Gnostic concept of the Supreme Being. If Jehovah created the world, as represented by the Old Testament, then Jehovah could not have been a perfect being. They rejected most of the Bible and opposed most of the doctrinal positions that were adopted by Christianity.

Gnosticism was so speculative in nature that each important leader was likely to adopt quite different concepts and employ different terminology. This resulted in almost endless Gnostic parties, each known by its founder.

Manichaeism, named for Mani, a Mesopotamian, conceived the idea of blending Oriental dualism and Christianity into a harmonious whole, and to substitute other Eastern concepts for the Jewish elements in Christianity. Mani regarded himself as an apostle of Jesus, and also the promised Paraclete (or Holy Spirit). This was an extreme form of Gnosticism, emphasizing the Oriental elements.

Through the second century and part of the third, teachers with lesser degrees of Gnostic tendencies carried forward their propaganda as members of regular Christian churches, winning to their point of view many of the more intelligent members. For example, Marcion, a native of Pontus went to Rome about A.D. 138 and became a member of the Roman church. He was almost wholly free from the speculative spirit that permeated the Egyptian and the Syrian Gnostics and did not exalt knowledge above faith. He accepted the Old Testament as the revelation of the God of the Jews, but he declared that Jehovah could not be the same as the God of the New Testament. He attempted to bring the Roman church to his way of thinking, but failed in the effort and felt constrained to organize his adherents into a separate church to continue in the propagation of his views.

Theodotus sought to expound his views in the Roman church about 190. According to an anonymous writer (possibly Hippolytus), Theodotus believed in the supernatural birth of Christ, but insisted that Christ was a "mere man" until His baptism, at which time the Holy Spirit bestowed upon him divine attributes. This form of doctrine, known as Adoptionism, was condemned by the Roman Church.

Paul of Samosata, Bishop of Antioch A.D. 260 and onward, like Theodotus, insisted that God is one person, rejecting the Trinity. He regarded Jesus as a divinely begotten man, energized by the Holy Spirit, and the Savior of men, yet he refused to identify Him with the Eternal Christ (or Logos).

Praxeas and Noetus, both from Asia Minor, sought to propagate the view that God the Father and the Son were not only indistinguishable, but were absolutely the same personality. They did not hesitate to say of God the Father whatever was considered true of God in the flesh (or Christ), and therefore, would say that God was born, God died, and suffered.

A disciple of Noetus propagated his views in Rome, and Hippolytus speaks of the "Heresy of Noetus," and according to him, Zephyrinus, Bishop of Rome, and his successor, Callistus, secretly aided in the spread of the propaganda.

LEGALISTIC SECTS

Montanism began in Phrygia sometime between A.D. 135 and 160. Montanus, along with two women, claimed to have been especially enlightened by the Holy Spirit and commissioned to announce a kingdom of Christ on earth, and to denounce the laxity against worldliness in the churches.

They claimed to receive special divine revelation, in a state of ecstasy, and supposed that in themselves was fulfilled the saying of Christ that when the Spirit of Truth comes, "he will guide you into the whole truth...." Montanism was a legalistic Christian movement in the spirit of the Judaizers, bent toward making religion a matter of the performance of outward observances.

To them, second marriages were equivalent to adultery; they rejected the use of wine, insisted on long and frequent fasting, and believed that flight from persecution or denial of the faith, whatever the occasion, was a mortal and unpardonable sin.

The Novationists arose in the spirit of the Montanists after the Decian persecutions of A.D. 250 and opposed receiving back into the churches multitudes of those who had denied the faith in the face of persecution. Most churches were in favor of readmitting "traditors," but the Novationists opposed the laxity and often withdrew from the churches when they failed to win their point.

The Donatists followed in the legalistic footsteps of the Montanists and Novationists and were active in the wake of the Diocletian persecutions near the end of the fourth century. They were distinguished for their earnestness and zeal, and their protests against corruption were entirely justified, but the spirit of their protests seems to have been more hopelessly contrary to the true spirit of Christianity than those they opposed. They opposed Mensurius, Bishop of Carthage, who sought to avoid persecution or death, and was using all of his influence against the fanatic practice of Christians to needlessly throw themselves into the hands of the persecutors. The Donatists were condemned in a council that met at Carthage in 411. A fierce persecution followed, but was ended by the invasion of the Vandals.

As worldliness and corruption in the churches increased, reactionary parties continued to rise up in opposition until they finally withdrew from the churches and the spirit of their movement ended in monasticism.

THE GREAT DOCTRINAL CONTROVERSIES

It was undoubtedly hoped that when organized Christianity had gained the power to enforce its decisions, controversy would be ended. Yet, never had controversy raged so fiercely as in the fourth and following centuries. The disputes already raging came forth with even greater zeal, and new conflicts arose. Persecution of the less powerful was employed without scruple, but did little to diminish the persistence of their squabbles. The persecuted parties only seemed to multiply and spread.

Doctrinal questions were raised over many issues, mostly by Eastern bishops and monks, whose never-ending desire was to work out more precise definitions. There were some who held to the opinion that the Son of God is equal to the Father. Those who held this opinion were accused of worshipping two gods. Others made a distinction between the Father and the Son, saying that Christ is not eternal and not equal to God, or not of the same substance, or is a created being.

In the minds of some, the Father and the Son were so fused into one divine being that it could be said that "God died" when Christ was crucified, and that Mary could be called the "Mother of God." Opinions varied as to whether Christ had a human soul and upon how much emphasis was to be placed on His humanity.

The influence of the Gnostics continued to live and continued to promote the heresy that God could not have created such an evil world, and that He must remain far removed and without connection with sinful humanity.

THE ARIAN CONTROVERSY
(ON THE GODHEAD)

Arius, a presbyter in the church of Alexandria, was not satisfied with any doctrinal statements of the relationship of God the Father to the Son. He held that the Son is a created being, and although not divine, is far above humankind and deserves to be worshipped. He declared that:

> "We must either suppose two divine original essences without beginning and independent of each other ... or we must not shrink from asserting that the Logos (Christ, the Word) had a beginning of his existence - that there was when He was not."

The problem was to distinguish between God, the Father, and the Son without denying the divinity of

Christ, and to say that Christ is divine without saying that there are two Gods. Is the Son a created being and, therefore, not eternal and not in the highest sense divine, or is He eternal, truly God, of the same essence, but with a personality distinct from that of the Father?

Arius was a man of pure and ascetical life, and his influence in Alexandria soon began to be felt. In 321, a synod was called which deposed him from the presbyterate and excluded him from communion with the church. The result was a schism (or division) which soon spread far and wide.

By the time Constantine called the Nicene Council to settle the controversy; the idea of the absoluteness of the Christian religion had taken strong hold upon the Christian consciousness. Christianity could not long remain content with any statement that involved the subordination of its head. If Christianity be the absolute religion, then Christ must be regarded as absolutely divine. It was, therefore, no accident that the doctrine of the absolute divinity of Christ should have prevailed and become part and parcel of the Christianity of the subsequent ages.

THE PERSON OF CHRIST
(CHRISTOLOGY)

Very little effort had been made during the first three centuries to analyze the person of Christ. Origen was probably the first to say distinctly that Christ had a human soul, this being in accord with his theory that Christ became a man to save men, and an angel to save angels. Whether Christ had both a completely human nature and a completely divine nature was not the foremost question of the day, but it was brought to the front by a monk named Nestorius.

Nestorius, a devout, learned, and eloquent monk, was presbyter of the church of Antioch and in 428 was made patriarch of Constantinople. There, he found many erroneous expressions and modes of thought being circulated in the church.

Especially offensive to him was the term, "Mother of God," as applied to Mary, the mother of Jesus. The expression, first used by Noetus and his followers, and introduced to the church at Rome early in the third century, came more directly to Nestorius from a theory of Apollinaris (about 370) that in Christ was the complete union of the divine and human natures, not as wholly God and wholly man, but rather as a mixture of God and man, completely fused into one personality, so that he did not hesitate to say that "God died," or that "God was born, etc.

This theory once clearly stated aroused much opposition among many churches, just as it did at Constantinople, but a fierce advocate of the theory was found in Cyril, patriarch of Alexandria, who was always eager to humiliate the patriarchs of Antioch and Constantinople.

It was decided that Nestorius and Cyril would lay their views before Coelestin, Bishop of Rome, who had reason to be predisposed against Nestorius. A Roman synod was convened in 430 which condemned Nestorius and ordered him to recant his statements on pain of excommunication. Cyril warned the bishops of Constantinople and other Eastern churches against the errors of Nestorius, and used every means at his disposal to arouse hostility against him.

The emperor (at Constantinople) was suspicious of Cyril and accused him of meddling in the affairs of both the imperial court and of the patriarch, and when propositions and counter propositions were issued by other parties, the emperor saw no other way than to call a general council.

The Council of Ephesus met in 431. A large body of fanatical monks were ready to carry out any riotous measure that Cyril might suggest, but Nestorius consistently refused to sit in council with the fanatical mob. Cyril's party met without the sanction of the imperial commissioner. They deposed Nestorius, and anathematized (or condemned) his doctrines. Some days after the proceedings, John, of Antioch, a supporter of Nestorius, arrived, met with his own thirty-two bishops and a few others in council, and excommunicated Cyril and the bishop of Ephesus who supported Cyril.

Both parties were strictly prohibited from visiting Constantinople to seek an advantage from the emperor, but Cyril was able to enlist the help of an aged monk who had lived in solitude for 48 years, and who, after being aroused to fanatical zeal by Cyril, was able to march to the imperial palace with an immense torch-lighted parade of monks and abbots from the cloisters.

This was the turning point in favor of Cyril. His agents were admitted into the imperial presence, and eventually the emperor saw that the popular feeling was too strong against Nestorius to allow him to continue his position of patriarch, and therefore, "allowed him to retire to the cloister."

Cyril triumphed over Nestorius, but he was held responsible for the prevailing turmoil. In 433, under imperial pressure and after considerable negotiation, he agreed to sign a creed in which the term "Mother of God" was applied to Mary in a somewhat limited sense.

The attempted settlement accomplished nothing, for in about 444 the dispute was revived in an intensified form in the Eutychian controversy, after the death of Cyril. At that time, the learned Theodoret assumed the leadership of the Antiochian party and, by his wonderful tact, was able to argue convincingly that the position of Eutyches (who took up the case for Cyril) represented God as suffering the frailties of humanity that Christ, himself, suffered.

A Synod held at Constantinople in 448 took a position substantially the same as Theodoret's, and Eutyches was charged with holding extreme views and refusing to admit to two natures in the incarnate Christ.

The Council of Chalcedon which convened 451 made a decision based on a letter from Pope Leo to Emperor Flavian. It basically upheld the position of the Antiochians, but was characteristic of Western theology in its practical character and lack of delicate distinctions. It recognized elements of truth in both sides of the argument without following either to its extreme consequences. Leo's position clearly stated for the first time both the true humanity and the true divinity of the incarnate Christ that came together as two complete natures in one person. It was an important victory and a great credit to the Roman Church that this formula should have proceeded from a Roman bishop.

SIN AND GRACE

Another great controversy had much to do with the temperaments and personalities of Augustine and Pelagius of the fifth century. They developed radical differences in their conceptions of human nature and the nature of God through their own experiences.

Augustine was tempestuous and passionate. The excesses and irregularities of his youth and early manhood were to him a lifelong subject of regret. His ideas of human depravity were derived from his experiences related to Paul's description of the antagonism between the flesh and the spirit, and between the intentions of the mind and the demands of the body. Augustine almost lost sight of the freedom of man in his contemplations of the absoluteness of God.

Pelagius, on the other hand, was a learned monk of cold, even temperament, leading a life of abstinence. To him it seemed easy to live uprightly. He was conscious of freedom to perform the dictates of his higher nature and saw no need of supposing that Adam's posterity had inherited his guilt. To him, man seemed fully equipped by nature for living a life of righteousness by using such help as God is willing to give to all.

The teachings of Pelagius failed to win broad acceptance by the Christian world, and it would be many centuries before the teachings of Augustine would be the dominant theology. Augustine placed too much stress on the inner Christian life and too little stress on external ceremonies to suit the spirit of the age. His teachings were radically opposed to the sacramental system of the day and to the idea of salvation by external works. He was an earnest advocate of asceticism, but denied that the torture of the flesh produces spiritual benefits. The world would wait long for Luther and Calvin, the true successors of Augustine.

THE QUESTION OF IMAGES

During the First, Second, and Third Centuries, Christians rejected with abhorrence anything like image worship. They were reproached by the pagans as atheists because they had no images and were, therefore, thought to have no gods. Pagans answered to charges of image worship, saying that they worshipped, not the images, but the gods that the images represent. Christians asked them why then did they not turn their eyes toward heaven.

The Synod of Elvira in 302 decreed that "pictures ought not to be in the churches." The decree, in itself, is evidence that pictures had already begun to be revered among some Christians. Men of influence came from paganism to Christianity and, being often appointed to high office, brought their image worship and other accustomed practices into the Church, although, as it was said, the images were not to be actually worshipped.

With the favor of the monastic system, for which the use of images seems quite suitable, their use continued to increase. By the seventh century, such worship had become so prevalent that Christians were reproached by Jews and Muslims as idolaters.

The Muslims, by the early eighth century, had established themselves firmly in Palestine, Syria, and Armenia. Then in 723 Jezid, the Caliph, (Muslim ruler) commanded the removal of all pictures from Christian churches within his realm, and the effect of this order extended into Asia Minor. Leo, the Isaurian, Emperor, 718-741, looked upon image-worship not only as an abomination, but as a major obstacle in the conversion of the Jews and Muslims.

In order to promote peace with the Muslims, Leo, with the encouragement of several bishops, issued a decree prohibiting prostration before images and eliminating the use of images throughout the empire. He further directed that images be placed in positions so high that people could not kiss them.

When this decree was put into practice, it met with much opposition and was the occasion of many bloody riots. The monks, who were much given to idolatry and who dedicated much of their time to the painting of religious pictures, were chief fomenters of insurrection.

Pope Gregory II in the West, around 730, wrote Leo, reproaching him for placing "stumbling blocks before the weak ones" and urged him to trust the judgment of the councils and the *Fathers* rather than his own ignorance.

Leo responded that the six general councils said nothing about image-worship. He declared his supremacy in both civil and religious affairs and threatened to destroy the image of St. Peter at Rome and imprison the pope.

In 731, a Roman synod, under Gregory III, responded to the threat by passing a decree of excommunication against "anyone whomsoever that should thenceforth remove, destroy, or injure the images of Mary, Christ, or the saints." Leo, again, retaliated by cutting off certain revenues and annexing churches of Illyria (modern Yugoslavia) to the patriarchate of Constantinople

Leo's son, Constantine V, also sought to abolish image-worship and carried on a ruthless extermination of all ecclesiastics and monks who refused to renounce the practice, but Irene, the wife of Leo IV, the next emperor, who died after five years, was able to devise and carry out her own plans to restore image worship when their nine-year-old son became Constantine VI.

In 787 Irene convened the Second Nicene Council, composed of bishops who, under her influence, had all made up their minds to confess their sins and declare that, indeed, the Scriptures and the *Fathers* do teach that the use of images is consistent with apostolic tradition.

The council attempted to make the position appear reasonable by their interesting distinction in a decree that "bowing down to and kissing," are not the same as "worshipping." The former was approved for images, and the latter was said to be reserved for God alone. Image-worship was thus once more established in the East, but only for a few years.

In 813, Leo the Armenian became emperor, and by 815 the decrees of the Second Nicene Council were declared Null and Void. Theodora, who came to power in 842, reenacted the decrees, and once more restored the images to the churches and carried out a severe persecution. The Eastern practice was settled when a restriction was put into place that rigorously limited the images to pictures and mosaics, ruling out 3-dimensional figures.

In the West, Charlemagne, aided by his theologians, published the "Four Caroline Books" in which he condemned the Second Nicene Council. He scorned the idea that images are necessary for perpetuating the memory of holy places, as held by the image worshippers, and he condemned the image "breakers," maintaining that images are useful for the ornamentation of the churches and for the perpetuation of holy deeds. Since that time the Western Church has given free scope to the use of both paintings and sculpture.

THE ASCETIC SPIRIT

As long as persecution of Christians continued, there would be opportunity for self-denial in enduring hardships for the faith. In some sects, particularly those under Gnostic influence, the ascetic spirit was thoroughly perverted.

From the true Christian idea that those who would come after Christ must deny themselves, Christians of some sects came to look upon suffering as meritorious in itself, and many continued self-inflicted punishment long after persecution had ceased.

The tendency was intensified by the increase of worldliness in the churches. Many came to feel that it was impossible to live a truly Christian life in the worldly churches and withdrew from society to retire into the wastelands or caves of the mountains. There they spent their time in fasting and prayer and attempting to make the spirit triumph over the flesh.

The greater the rigor of self-discipline, the greater was considered to be the merit. Endless means of self-torture and extreme austerities were devised that ofttimes brought about insanity or death.

EARLY EVANGELICALS

The rapid rate at which evangelical parties spread over Europe and the hearty reception given to evangelical preachers by the common people during the Middle Ages suggest that traces of evangelical life had survived from an earlier time.

THE "PROTESTANTS OF THE EAST"

In the seventh and eighth centuries there were tales being told of persons returning from captivity in the near East bringing with them copies of the New Testament and the determination to devote all their efforts to restoring Christianity to its original form. There may have been some truth to those tales, for the Paulicians had existed in those areas for several centuries, and their beliefs and practices, as shown in the "Key of Truth," seem to be much in accord with the Christianity of a very early time, before extensive corruption of doctrine and practice had taken place.

The name "Paulician" was probably derived, not from Paul the Apostle, but from Paul of Samosata, who became bishop of Antioch in 260 and was excommunicated by a great provincial synod in 269 for holding to the adoptionist doctrine of the divinity of Christ (apparently influenced by Gnostic thinking). The doctrine, discussed earlier, was based on the belief that Jesus was begotten of Mary by the Holy Spirit, not as divine and eternal, but as an ordinary man, and that he remained an ordinary man until He was energized with divine attributes as the Holy Spirit descended upon Him at His baptism.

Some writers have tried to stigmatize Paul of Samosata with holding to Gnostic dualism, but Adoptionist language was often used by otherwise orthodox teachers due to the fact that the doctrine of the person of Christ had not yet been made the subject of exhaustive study, and the logical consequences of such language were not understood. Such efforts to stigmatize certain individuals were doubtless due to the unscrupulous practices of the time, when it was not unusual that the most damaging accusations would be made against opponents.

Adoptionism is known to have become the prevailing type of Christianity in Armenia, where its practice was not so much a fundamental doctrine as it was a means of combating the Eastern doctrines of the nature of Christ, the worship of Mary and the saints, image worship, and all the intolerance, and moral corruption of the system.

The doctrines and practices of the Paulicians from about the eighth century forward found in the "Key of Truth," confirms that they were opposed to infant baptism and practiced believer's baptism for those of maturity and understanding. A translation of a passage on baptism from "The Key of Truth" reads:

> "Therefore, according to the word of the Lord, we must first bring them unto the faith, and then give it (baptism) unto them.... For they (those who learned from the Lord) first taught; secondly, asked for faith; thirdly, induced to repent; and after that, granted holy baptism to those who were of full age, and in particular were cognizant of their original sin...."

The Supper, they called "the mystery of salvation," and the "blessed" bread and wine, they said, were "changed into His (Christ's) body and blood." It is not known if these statements were intended to mean the real presence of the body and blood of Christ or if it was meant in the spiritual sense, but undoubtedly, like baptism, it was observed as a very solemn occasion.

The Paulician movement included many races of Southern and Eastern Europe and Africa, and they all found refuge in the "huge recess or circular dam" formed by the Taurus Mountain Range of Armenia. This refuge provided comparative security from persecution from both the Greek and Roman forms of Christianity throughout the more exposed parts of Armenia.

They did, however, suffer severe persecution from time to time, and under Empress Theodora, a hundred thousand of the Paulicians are said to have been massacred about A.D. 844. With the capture of their stronghold, their power was broken and a mighty barrier against the advance of the Muslims was destroyed.

The Paulicians settled in vast colonies in Thrace and Bulgaria. They leavened Eastern Europe with Christianity, and were undoubtedly connected with the widespread Christian movement into Central and Western Europe from the eleventh century onward.

EARLY EVANGELICALS IN GREAT BRITAIN

Christianity came early to Great Britain, and it is highly likely that it was introduced by Roman soldiers. There are some indications of the influence of Irenaeus, who was bishop at Lyons, in Gaul for some time prior to his death in A.D. 185. By 314, Christianity had attained to considerable influence. Several British bishops sat in the Synod of Arles, and Britain was represented in the Council of Ariminium in 350. There is no evidence, however, that any Britons sat in the Nicene Council of 325.

After the Roman army was withdrawn, about 410, there was little contact between the Christians of Britain and those under the influence of Rome. About 449, the Angles, Saxons, Jutes, and others from the continent began to invade Britain and gradually forced the Christians westward into the more secure mountain hidings of Wales. Here they organized themselves in a semi-monastic way, perhaps perpetuating the Celtic clan system, and formed large communities, each presided over by an abbot (superior, as in a monastery). Each individual was assigned to the kind of work for which he was considered best suited, and large numbers devoted themselves to the study of the Bible.

When an effort was made to bring them under the subjection of Rome, about the close of the sixth century, they held firmly to their own practices. Information available about their peculiarities is scanty, but from their contacts with Roman emissaries, we understand that the British gave great attention to the study of the Scriptures and had numerous colleges for the promotion of Bible and Christian life studies.

They were unsurpassed in missionary zeal, and practiced it on several fronts throughout the fifth and sixth centuries, planting churches in Ireland, Scotland, the Netherlands, Germany, and Switzerland. It is worthy to note that the very regions in which their mission work thrived are the same regions where evangelical movements flourished in later times.

These British Christians insisted on humility and simplicity in Christian life and were offended by the pomp and worldliness of the Roman missionaries. While they were not in all respects apostolic, they did represent a form of early Christianity before the centralization of power in the head of the Church. They had no Episcopal practices; they absolutely refused to recognize human authority in matters of religion, and indignantly rejected all efforts to bring them into subjection to the bishop of Rome.

In 596, Gregory the Great, who before his elevation to the papacy (the office of the pope), had intended to go to Britain for the purpose of converting the Saxons, sent Augustine, a monk, with about thirty other missionary monks and Frankish interpreters.

By making a parade of ascetical life, pretended miracles, and promises of earthly advantages, they succeeded in converting Ethelbert, king of the Saxons, who with about ten thousand followers, received baptism in a river at the hands of the missionaries. A firm alliance was formed between the king and the papal office to secure the subjection of the British Christians to Rome.

When all other means accomplished nothing, the Saxon king was persuaded to launch an expedition against the British Christians. Three thousand were slaughtered on one occasion. For centuries the Christians of the old British type, in Wales, Scotland, Ireland, and parts of Germany, resisted with all their might the encroachment of Rome, and perhaps some descendants survived into later centuries.

The methods employed by Augustine had the smell of treachery, and Ethelbert, no doubt, had concluded that deceit for a good cause is excusable. By 601, a thorough organization of the Roman type of Christianity had been in place and Augustine had been made archbishop.

Within a few years, a well-organized and well-equipped state Church, enthusiastically devoted to Rome and the pope, had been developed in the extensive Saxon dominions. Large numbers of monasteries had been formed in which zeal for learning and enthusiasm was equal to the older British type.

Nowhere during the seventh and eighth centuries was the Roman Church so vigorous and aggressive as in Britain. It was the Anglo-Saxon monasteries that sent most of the great missionaries that evangelized the continent of Europe, and it was to them that Charlemagne was to look for his educational leaders.

GNOSTIC INFLUENCES IN WESTERN EUROPE

The presence of the Saracens (Arabs, without Sarah) in Spain was favorable to the development of certain Oriental heresies. In 991, Gerbert, who later became Pope Sylvester II, on being consecrated as Archbishop of Rheims, took occasion to denounce certain Gnostic errors.

The Cathari heresy is said to have been brought from Italy by a certain woman who led many people astray. As a consequence, ten clergymen were burned for heresy in Orleans in 1022.

The two separate groups of the heresy agreed in ascribing the Old Testament to the prince of evil. They agreed that Christ's body was only an appearance, but nevertheless, Christ ate, drank, and experienced suffering, and both parties laid great stress on the laying-on-of-hands in a ceremony called the *Consolamentum*.

The *Consolamentum* was to be used by those that were already sanctified, to impart the Holy Spirit and salvation to others. The ceremony was used after a long period of training in which the most solemn promises of fidelity and secrecy were made.

It laid great stress on the laying-on-of-hands that took place in the waters of baptism and was ordinarily postponed to the deathbed to allow more freedom for an individual to mingle in the world until just before he was expected to enter the future life. Then was the time to have his sins forgiven.

To be sure that the efforts of the Consolamentum were not wasted, there was the Endura, which involved the withholding of food from those who might otherwise recover. Death was often preferred at that time, as the subject felt secure in being fully prepared.

THE EMPIRE OF CHARLEMAGNE

Charles, one of the sons of Pepin and afterward known as Charlemagne, after serving jointly with his brother for twenty-four years, succeeded in vastly extending the Frankish domains. He carried out the policy that Pepin had made by treaty with the papacy. He felt that it was the duty of the state to honor and protect the Church and discipline it, if need be, and that it was the duty of the Church to aid the state in maintaining unity and order.

The growth of papal power went hand-in-hand with that of Charlemagne, and the Church had the full support of the civil arm in its effort to overcome heresy and paganism. A firm alliance had long existed between the Frankish rulers on the one hand and the pope on the other, and Charlemagne had become seized with the idea of a Holy Roman Empire, working as partners with the Holy Catholic Church, each having world-wide dominion in its own sphere, bringing peace and the blessings of civilization to all mankind.

The grandeur of the Roman Empire, and the stability for which it stood, had made a profound impression on the Teutonic people. With the virtual extinction of the authority of the Eastern Empire in Italy and the growth of the Franks, it was natural that the greatest of all the Frankish rulers, having been invited again and again to guard the papal estates from the Lombards, and having become the virtual ruler of Italy, should think of himself as a successor with the dignity and name of the Roman Emperor. Charlemagne was eager to gain all the power and prestige that the pope could place upon him.

In 799, Pope Leo III was driven from Rome by a hostile faction. He called upon Charlemagne, who assisted him in regaining his authority. By 800, Charlemagne had established peace and tranquility throughout his vast realm and returned to Rome to secure recognition as the successor of the Caesars. On Christmas day, A.D. 800, he was crowned by the pope and given the name Roman Emperor.

The Holy Catholic Church and the Holy Roman Empire were regarded as the counterpart of one another, and each had before it the dominion of the world as its goal. They would work hand-in-hand toward that end. The missionaries of the Church had the full support of the civil government for overthrowing heresy.

Charlemagne worked diligently for the revival of learning. He brought to Gaul the best of scholars from Britain, or wherever they could be found, and provided a great stimulus to education. This proved highly advantageous to the Church, as the work of education was left entirely in the hands of the clergy.

During the reign of Emperor Louis the Pius, Charlemagne's son, Gregory IV (827-844), a feeble pope, was used by unscrupulous churchmen for perpetrating upon Christendom a body of spurious documents.

The immediate purpose was to overthrow Louis the Pious, Constantine's son, in favor of a grandson, but Gregory was reluctant to take extreme measures against "so pious an emperor." The abbot of a convent overcame Gregory's scruples by showing him documents that were reported to be based on the authority of "his own holy predecessors." These documents made some very bold claims regarding the powers of the pope. Among other things, it was declared that:

> "In him dwelt the fullness of that living power which came down from God and the Apostle Peter, whereby he was ordained to be judge of all men and of all things; and in such wise that he himself should be judged of no man."

Gregory no longer hesitated to complete the overthrow of Louis and to recognize the grandson as emperor, and did so in 833. Contemporaries fittingly applied the term "The Field of Lies" to this transaction and others that were to follow. The weakness and subserviency of Louis the Pius encouraged the hierarchy to perform one of the most magnificent forgeries of history. Beginning with those presented to Pope Gregory, a vast body of spurious decretals and quotations from the *early fathers*, called the Pseudo-Isidorian decretals by historians, was imposed upon Christendom.

Many older forgeries, the "Donation of Constantine," the "Canons of the Apostles," the "Letters of Clement to James," and others were made a part of this collection along with some decretals of the popes of the second and third centuries. These documents set forth the fully developed claims of the hierarchy, and although the forgeries likely did not originate with Rome, Rome was not slow to put them into practice.

Pope Nicholas I (858-867) used to the fullest the teachings and implications of the Pseudo-Isidorian Decretals and was prepared to wage a relentless warfare against any that should impugn the absolute sovereignty and irresponsibility of his office. He enforced the right of lay persons and the lower echelons of the hierarchy the right of appeal to Rome and would at times take advantage of these appeals in order to humiliate archbishops for failing to recognize the pope's authority as being higher than the authority of provincial synods.

THE GROWTH OF CORRUPTION

As the empire established under Charlemagne was approaching its end, the state of the papacy suffered along with the general degeneration of society. Never was it more degraded than from 880 to 1000. After the empire dissolved, Europe lapsed into anarchy, and Italy was torn into fragments by contending factions.

Offices of bishops and monasteries were seized upon by warring nobles for their sons. Those thus appointed were anything other than pious or learned in theology. The papacy lost its prestige and came to be a point of contention between rival factions.

Pope Formosus (891-898), after being the victim of some particular indignity, forthwith wreaked bloody vengeance upon the enemy. He was then apparently poisoned. During the next five years, one pope reigned for fifteen days, another was strangled after a year. One lasted four months, one lasted three weeks, and one lasted about four years. Leo V, in 903, after he had reigned for two months, was murdered by his chaplain. The chaplain was murdered and was succeeded by Sergius III after eight months of pontifical glory.

With Sergius was inaugurated what is known in history as the *Pornocracy*. Upon his death, the office of the pope was run by his mistresses for seven years. One of his mistresses appointed the next pope, who was strangled by another mistress, Marozia. The next three popes were the sons of Marozia. The third, being fathered by Pope Sergius and became Pope John XI.

From 936 to 956, a sort of Roman Republic prevailed, with Alberic as emperor. He appointed four popes in succession and restrained them from political interference. A son of Alberic, a youth profligate beyond his years, succeeded his father in the civil government and then assumed the papal office, himself, as John XII.

He was charged with the violation of almost every principle of morality and religion, including the invoking of Jupiter and Venus, living with his father's mistress, and turning the papal palace into a brothel. John was driven from the city by the German emperor, Otto[54] the Great, at the request of the people. He was tried under Otto, but after a time was restored through the intervention of some of his ladies.

THE GERMANIC EMPIRE AND THE POLICY OF REFORM

The authority of Otto was increasing, and he was trying to bring order out of chaos. He secured control in Italy in 962, assumed responsibility for the appointment of the popes, and began to deliver the papacy from the debasing position into which it had fallen. Following the example of Charlemagne, Otto sought to strengthen his imperial authority by receiving the anointment of the pope, who happened to be the disreputable John XII.

Otto is said to have solemnly promised to exalt both the Church of Rome and her pastor and to protect them in the enjoyment of their dignities and territorial possessions. The tradition of past greatness was preserved with the revival of the Holy Roman Empire by Otto, and the papacy entered upon a career of brilliant conquest.

When John's vicious life was brought to his attention, Otto treated the matter lightly. He expressed the hope that with increasing age John would learn to conduct himself with more propriety. When he learned, however, that John was negotiating to have the Greeks and Hungarians invade Italy and expel the Germans, that was a serious matter, and he proceeded immediately to capture Rome.

---

[54]Or Otho

In 963 Otto convoked a synod of bishops and cardinals to depose the pope and to appoint a successor. The new pope took office under the name of Leo VIII. With the approval of the synod, Leo issued a decree recognizing the right of Otto and his successors to nominate future rulers of Italy and to appoint future popes, bishops, and archbishops. Otto I died in 973, and Italy relapsed into anarchy. The office of the pope shared the same fate.

In 999 Otto III regained control and appointed one of the most learned men of the time as pope under the name of Sylvester II. Sylvester had received his education under Arabian scholars and was so far in advance of his contemporaries that he was suspected of practicing witchcraft. He was the first pope, as far as is known, to propose a crusade for the deliverance of the Holy Sepulcher from the hands of the Saracens (without Sarah, meaning Arabians).

Otto III shared the grave apprehension that the close of the first millennium would bring the end of the world, but the year 1000 passed without catastrophe, and there was universal rejoicing.

For the next half-century, a succession of three emperors pursued the general policy of church reform, promoting men to ecclesiastical office on the ground of merit and attempting to institute vigorous measures for reforming the church, but the Italian clergy proved irreformable. There, benefices (positions with guaranteed benefits) were sold in reckless abandon, and licentiousness was rampant.

Emperor Henry III, in his zeal for reform, called a synod at Sutri in 1046, summoned Pope Gregory VI, and deposed him for simony (buying the office). He appointed a "respectable" German bishop to the position under the name of Clement II.

In 1049, Bruno, bishop of Torel, Henry's uncle was elevated to the papacy as Leo IX. Bruno forthwith appointed Hildebrand as sub-deacon and administrator of the Patrimony of Peter (the distribution of endowments and entitlements). With the cooperation of the emperor, strenuous measures were entered upon for the abolition of simony and immorality among the clergy. Many of the more upright among the clergy rejoiced in his well-directed efforts and gave their hearty cooperation.

HILDEBRAND'S SCHEME OF REFORM

As the Roman hierarchy gradually regained its power under the fostering care of the emperors, a new party came forth under the leadership of Hildebrand, which resented civil interference in matters of religion. This party sought to free the Church from civil authority by centralizing all its powers in the office of the pope.

Hildebrand emerged from his education as a monk, full of ambition. He was assigned, first, as chaplain to Gregory VI, then, in 1049, became sub-deacon and cardinal under Leo IX. From then on he controlled papal policy as chief statesman in the office of the pope. He could have, on several occasions, secured the election to the papacy himself, but he preferred to labor in a subordinate position up to 1073, when he assumed the tiara under strong pressure.

Hildebrand became, unquestionably, the greatest ecclesiastical statesman of the Middle Ages. He identified papal supremacy in the most absolute way with the will of God and allowed nothing to stand in the way of achieving his ideal of universal papal dominion in both the spiritual and the secular domains. His able literary defender Peter Damiani maintained:

> "that every invasion of the prerogative of the Roman Church is heresy and should be dealt with as such; that all law, even the law of God, Himself, may be set aside, if this should be deemed by the Church necessary for the accomplishment of its purposes; that the divine law bends to the immediate needs or interests of the Church; that the present interests of the Church, as judged by the Church, represent God's will and must be secured, even if the violation of God's will otherwise expressed be involved; that the Church may and should violate any compacts made with civil rulers if contrary to the interests of the Church."

With a shrewdness rarely equaled, and a boldness of conception and action never surpassed, Hildebrand, as Pope Gregory VII, set to work to utilize the reforming spirit of the time for the building up of ecclesiastical authority.

His aim was to take disciplinary power out of the hands of civil rulers and to use it for the complete subjugation of the clergy and laity to the will of the pope.

In the face of the gravest difficulties in opposing the clergy, he remorselessly enforced the law of celibacy. Married clergy were stigmatized to be the same, or worse, than those who kept concubines; the people were forbidden to confess to them or to receive religious service of any kind from them.

Where there was a reluctance to obey, monks were commissioned to go into parishes and to arouse popular sentiment against recalcitrant clergy until they would either renounce their wives or would be forced to flee.

Bishops and abbots were forbidden to receive their appointments through lay influence. They must renounce any sort of dependence on lay patrons and submit themselves absolutely to the pope. Civil rulers were reluctant to abandon the patronage they had enjoyed from time immemorial, but against all the resistance, Hildebrand was for the most part able to make his point. The humiliation of Henry IV at Canossa became one of the most noted events in the history of the struggle of church and state for supremacy.

Henry had fought against a decree of the pope which forbade civil rulers from making appointments to church offices. He attempted to depose the pope, and for that he was excommunicated. His subjects forsook him, leaving him no choice other than to seek forgiveness for his rash deeds.

The story told was that the pope, being in a retreat in the mountains at the time, required Henry to stand barefoot in the snow for three days before being admitted to kneel at the pontiff's feet for pardon.

Hildebrand quoted the prophets which he thought applied, as he exhorted his subjects to renounce their allegiance to Henry IV:

> "If thou declare not unto the wicked his evil way, his blood will I require at thy hand;"

and again:

> "Cursed be he that withholdeth the sword from blood."

and he added:

> "for we are clearly taught by the holy fathers that he upon whom the duty resteth, yet neglecteth to resist the wicked man, in reality consenteth unto the evil, and (he) himself commits the sin it was his duty to punish."

Defending his right to excommunicate princes, citing a number of false decretals, he goes on to say,

> "But perhaps there are persons who will pretend that when God thrice committed his church to the blessed Peter by the words 'feed my sheep,' he made kings an exception. But let them reflect that when he gave to Peter the power to bind and loose in heaven and on earth, that he did not make any exceptions...."

Hildebrand wrote to William the Conqueror on the subject of papal prerogative that the Church was ordained to rule the civil powers:

> "...and Scripture teacheth that the apostolic and pontifical dignity is ordained to be responsible for all Christian kings, nay, for all men, before the divine tribunal, and to

render an account to God for their sins. If, therefore, I be answerable before the dreadful judgment seat, judge whether ye are not bound upon the peril of your soul ... to yield unto me unconditional obedience...."

To carry out his purposes, Hildebrand made full use of all the means of influence that had been made available to him from the past, such as the monastic orders, the admiration of asceticism, popular superstitions, and forged decretals that were intended to legitimize the supreme power of the pope.

Hildebrand's system of well-trained monks, who faithfully represented him, allowed him to be virtually omnipresent in all matters related to the Church. Yet his triumph was far from complete. Henry IV did not long remain in the same state of mind as when he was standing in the snow at Canossa. He soon captured Rome and drove the pope from the throne. Characteristic of Hildebrand, he said in his dying words that he died in exile "because I have always loved righteousness and hated iniquity."

GOD'S "REPRESENTATIVE ON EARTH"

The ablest and, by far, the most successful of all popes was Innocent III, who came to the office at a most favorable time. He had the work of Hildebrand and other advocates of absolute papal rule behind him and the crusades brought immense authority and vast resources to the Church. Canon Law (the law of the

Church) was fully developed, and the great intellectual activity that resulted from the Crusades was manifesting itself in the founding of universities, a chief object of which was the defense of Church dogma.

Innocent had completely grasped the idea of absolute civil and ecclesiastical control. He approached more nearly to realization of this idea than any other pope was able to do, and he was the first pope to designate himself "the representative of God on earth."

THE CRUSADES

Dominant during the Middle Ages was a religion of form and ceremony, and superstition abounded. The awe and respect given to shrines and relics and the belief in their capacity to work miracles and to confer spiritual benefits was almost universal.

From the fifth century onward, pilgrimages to the Holy Land and to the Holy Sepulcher had been regarded as the surest way to acquire merit and to atone for the most grievous of sins. Christians had been guaranteed by early Moslem rulers the right to visit the holy places without molestation. Pilgrims, without purse or script, often set out on foot to beg their way to Palestine, fully confident that loss of life in such an enterprise would result in immediate entrance into heavenly bliss.

The conversion of Hungary, around 997, opened up an overland route and tended to multiply the number of pilgrims. In 1095, the Greek emperor, sorely beset by the Turks, sent ambassadors to the Council of Piacenza to pray for the aid of Western Christendom. Pope Urban II was profoundly intrigued by the possibilities that lay in coming to the aid of an emperor in need. He could visualize extending the dominion of his Church and at the same time perform a service of great merit.

Urban and Peter the Hermit, both, appeared at the Council of Clermont in the same year. Peter had just returned from a pilgrimage and preached with consuming zeal. The pope also addressed the throng and aroused crusading enthusiasm to the point for immediate action. To all who would enlist, he promised the plenary remission of all the infinite penalties and penances they had accumulated by their past sins and the immediate protection of Peter, Paul, and the Holy Church. The multitude rose to their feet and cried out repeatedly, "It is the will of God! It is the will of God!" The pope then held before them the cross and called upon them to:

> "Wear it upon your shoulders and upon your breasts; let it shine upon your arms and upon your standards; it will be to you the surety of victory or the palm of martyrdom; it will unceasingly remind you that Christ died for you, and that it is your duty to die for him."

The symbol of the cross gave the name crusade to the movement. The pope proclaimed a *Truce of God* among the princes of Europe and bade them join the great effort for the rescue of the Holy Land. So great was the enthusiasm that great numbers were ready to obey. Insolvent debtors were liberated from their obligations. The prisons of Europe were emptied of all who would join the Crusade. The *Truce of God* was extended to embrace the full protection of the lives and belongings of all crusaders.

About six hundred thousand men, besides women and children, are said to have embarked on the first crusade. It was a disorganized host. Freed by their plenary indulgence from all moral obligations and compelled to support themselves on the populations through which they moved, they carried devastation everywhere.

Pestilence and famine rapidly reduced their numbers. Jerusalem was captured in 1099 by about forty thousand who were spared to participate in the glory, but they achieved only a temporary success. Godfrey of Bouillon, considered to be chief among the leaders, was proclaimed king, but he refused "wear the crown of royalty where Christ had worn a crown of thorns."

Bernard of Clairvaux, a monk, preacher, and mystical writer was chief promoter of the second crusade. It is said to have numbered well over one million fighting men and was a complete failure. When confronted with the failure of his prophecies, Bernard attributed the disaster to the guilt of the pilgrims.

Richard the Lion-hearted, king of England from 1189 to 1199, figured prominently in the third crusade which took place between 1190 and 1193, but it accomplished little. Richard, himself was taken captive and held for ransom for many years.

The fourth crusade, 1196-1197, resulted in complete defeat and a terrible massacre of the crusaders at Jaffa.

The fifth crusade, 1201-1204, was under the direction of Innocent III, the most powerful of all the popes. It expended most of its energy in gaining control of Constantinople and in establishing a Latin empire in order to bring the Eastern (Greek) Church into Obedience.

His attempt at coercion only served to intensify the alienation between the Eastern and Western Churches.

The Sixth Crusade was rendered fruitless by Emperor Frederick II, who was in no proper sense a crusader at all. His considerations were only political and personal gains, and he disregarded the interests of the pope in making treaties with the Saracens.

The next three crusades which took place in the following half-century can be characterized respectively as "fruitless," "without important results," and "almost completely destroyed." A children's crusade took place in 1212, in which thirty thousand French children, led by the boy Stephen, went forth under the enthusiasm of the time, they knew not whither. Multitudes died of exposure and hardship, and several thousand who made safe passage to the East were seized by the Arabs and sold into slavery.

A similar movement of twenty thousand boys and girls from Germany took place. About five thousand reached Genoa, where they had apparently expected that the waters of the sea would part as they took their first step into the water.

The ninth crusade embraced several feeble expeditions between 1259 and 1291. The crusading spirit was almost extinct, and the most desperate efforts to reawaken it proved futile, however, there were many crusades against heretics in Europe, such as against the Albigenses, 1208 to 1249, and against the Hussites from 1420 to 1431. These movements were accompanied by the indiscriminate massacre of the helpless populations in the regions invaded.

From the beginning, the popes recognized in the crusades a means of increasing their power and wealth. They argued that it was foolish for the provinces of Europe to fight among themselves while infidels were allowed to desecrate the Holy Land and the holy places. Thus, for two hundred years, the popes were at the head of a movement that was thoroughly popular and absorbed the attention of Christendom. Many an enthusiastic crusader, to make his salvation doubly sure, in case of his failure to return, bequeathed his entire estate to the Church.

This resulted in increasing the power and wealth of the pope, beyond comparison with any civil ruler. Long years of contact between the East and the West resulted in opening up commerce. Trade went hand in hand with manufacturing and changed the face of Europe. Feudalism began to yield to the establishment of great nations. The intellectual stimulation begun by contact with new ideas and strange sounding names and places indirectly resulted, in years to come, in the founding of great universities and the revival of learning.

The revival of learning, which was yet a great distance away, would come, but it must first overcome the formidable opposition of the dogmatic thinking of the day.

MEDIEVAL THEOLOGY

EARLY SCHOLASTICISM

A slight intellectual interest survived the period of the early Middle Ages, a period almost destitute of learning, but the Church could not allow freedom in the search for truth, since she, herself, already possessed the infallible truth by revelation. It would be necessary to limit freedom of thought, but there appeared to be a certain work of the intellect that could be done without causing a problem. It was to show that the infallible doctrines of the Church are rational and capable of being justified.

There was, however, a hidden danger that the Church would later discover - the danger that rational justification would become a requirement and that dogma would be measured by the test of logic.[55]

The word scholasticism (or the teachings of the schools) had long been used in Christian education to designate the formal theologizing conducted under the influence of a flawed translation of some of Aristotle's dialectic works. During the earlier Middle Ages, the method most often used in instruction was the recital of a series of pertinent passages from the *fathers* and decretals of the popes. Theology, along with all learning, was in a very degenerative state, and much of the knowledge of ancient civilizations had been lost.

The schools of Charlemagne had opened the door for the revival of learning, but learning had hardly begun when John Scotus Erigena, in 843 was invited by Charles the Bald to the headship of the Palatine school at Paris, a school patterned after those of Charlemagne.

Having knowledge of Greek, he was imposed upon to translate the Pseudo-Dionysian writings into Latin. These were writings that appeared in the fifth century that were claimed to have been written by Dionysius the Areopagite, converted under Paul's preaching at Athens, but they were in reality Neo-Platonic writings that taught a mixture of Plato and Christianity.

---

[55] A.K., Rogers, A Students history of Philosophy, pp.191-192

Erigena was greatly influenced, and the writings were largely influential in making the question of the *reality of universals*, espoused by Plato, the subject of the central philosophical debate of the Middle Ages. The question divided most of the thinkers into two great schools – the Realists (class terms are real) and the Nominalists (class terms are only a name).

The Realists, with Plato, held that class terms are timeless, perfect, and the pattern, or ideal thing, from which individual, and less perfect things, are made. Man, for example, is said to be more real than particular men, and as an ideal circle is the perfect pattern for individual circles, the ideal man is the perfect pattern, preexisting in the mind of God, for individual men.

The Nominalists, on the other hand, taking up the cause of common sense, denied such a concept and declared that it is the individuals, alone, that are real. Nominalism was bound to conflict with the whole principle of dogmatism, being a natural ally of the scientific spirit. It is compatible with the right and duty of investigation and considers skepticism as a condition of earnest research.

It was natural that the Church should be realistic. The graded system of reality in the intellectual world paralleled the hierarchy of the Roman ecclesiastical system. At the top, the pope stood supreme as the representative of the Church universal. To admit that the individual alone is real, and not the class, would have been to admit that particular churches have reality, while the one Holy Catholic Church is a mere name and that its mediation is not necessary for the soul's salvation.

Erigena set the example for later scholastic theologians by placing the *fathers* on the same level of authority as the Scriptures. According to him, "It is not for us to pass judgment on the wisdom of the *fathers*, but piously and reverently to accept their teachings...." He believed, however, that truth should be capable of a rational justification; therefore his philosophy fell short of fully developed scholasticism.

Anselm of Canterbury, a contemporary of Hildebrand, has been called the "Father of Scholasticism." He entertained none of the rationalistic tendencies as did Erigena, but insisted on unconditional submission to ecclesiastical authority, the benchmark of fully developed scholasticism.

FULLY-DEVELOPED SCHOLASTICISM

Sometime after the early ninth century, Arabian scholars translated into Arabic a number of writings of Greek philosophy, including those of Plato and Aristotle, as well as Neo-Platonist writings. Many of the Neo-Platonist writings were from the Syrian language and were translations that the Christians of Syria had previously translated for their own use.

On the basis of these writings, corrupted by the process of translation and re-translation, there grew up in the East, in North Africa, and in Spain, a Saracen (without Sara, Arabic) culture of which it was said that "The whole philosophy of the Arabians was only a form of Aristotelianism, tempered more or less with Neo-Platonic conception." The teachings of this culture became an influence upon Christian thinkers by the sojourn of Christian students into Arabic lands and by other contacts of the cultures and had much to do with the final result of fully developed scholasticism.

As Aristotle's authority (as it was understood), came to be given more weight, the work for the theological writer was to draw out, in a systematic form, as many conclusions as possible from each authoritative proposition.

Little significance was given to the practical value of the conclusions, and theology degenerated into idle hairsplitting, and sometimes into gross irreverence. The logical faculties of the mind were sharpened, but no fresh food for thought was produced. Outward forms were regarded as supremely important, and the spirit of Christianity suffered. There was no inducement to apply the intellect to the searching after truth by scientific methods.

To attempt to arrive at the exact teaching of the Scriptures by a study of the original languages, and by the application of other principles of interpretation, would have been regarded as an impertinence, and would have subjected a person to persecution for heresy.

Alexander of Hales, called the "Monarch of Theologians," was first to make full use of Aristotle's works as known through Arabic commentaries. He was a Franciscan, and agreed with the Order of *the Immaculate Conception* of the Mother of Jesus. He advocated withholding of the cup from the laity, and accepted sorrow for fear of being punished, as well as sorrow for sin, as sufficient for forgiveness.

Thomas Aquinas, the "Angelic Doctor," was the greatest of all scholastic theologians. He was a Dominican and upheld philosophical *realism* as a bulwark of orthodoxy. His work, *Summa Theologiae*, occupies the rank of the highest of its kind, and in it medieval thought is found in its most perfect form. More than any other scholastic theologian, he used the Scriptures, but only in such a way as to confirm the interpretations of the Church. His work represents the principle of absolute subserviency to ecclesiastical authority.

NOMINALISM

Roger Bacon, an Englishman, born about 1214, was educated in *scholastic theology*, but he differed greatly from Aquinas. He studied and understood the sciences with remarkable clearness for his age and is widely known today as "A man before his time, but his reward was to receive a reputation as a wizard or a magician.

His work was condemned by the Church, and late in his life he was confined for many years in prison. In spite of it all, his scientific spirit persisted and grew in strength, and in a later time, when the conditions were ripe, it became the compass for guiding the whole course of modern thought.

William Occam, who lived most of his life in the fourteenth century, took up the cause of the Nominalists in advocating the use of the inductive method for studying nature and the mind. He was, also, a most zealous advocate of religious and political reform.

THE INQUISITION

Much information about various factions of the Christianity of the past comes to us through their enemies, and that is especially true of the highly organized persecutions of the Middle Ages. Agents of the Inquisition, in the most organized of all persecutions, recorded confessions under the most excruciating circumstances to provide information to be used in other times and places in the inquisitorial process, thus leaving a record for posterity.

The theory had long prevailed that outside the church there is no salvation. Heresy was generally looked upon by churchmen as the greatest possible evil. and the toleration of heresy was looked upon as involving the gravest and most culpable neglect of duty.

As the organization of the hierarchy grew more complete, and as doctrine came to be more strictly defined, pressure increased to enforce uniformity in doctrine and practice. Aggressive and ambitious popes would vigorously insist upon greater diligence in the punishment of bishops and civil rulers accused of heresy. When heresy became so widespread and aggressive as to threaten the foundations of church authority, it was sure that measures for universal action would be adopted for its extermination. The heretic, as the enemy of God and man, was "worthy of no humane consideration."

It was during the papacy of Alexander III that the groundwork was laid for the Inquisition. The Council of the Lateran in 1179, while placing more emphasis on the prevention of simony and taking care of certain other matters, endeavored to unite Christendom in opposition to heresy, which was making alarming headway. Christian princes and people were called upon to take up arms and were assured of plenary indulgence (complete forgiveness of all sins) while engaged in the work of rooting it out.

From 1220 to 1239, Emperor Frederick II joined hands with the popes in the persecution of heresy. Laws were enacted that required those suspected to clear themselves of guilt or suffer the penalty of depravation of all civil rights. Obstinate heretics were condemned to the stake, and orders were given that their houses, and those of their friends, be destroyed and never rebuilt.

The lands of civil rulers who should neglect to drive out heresy were to be confiscated and placed under the control of someone who was willing to do so. Frederick placed at the disposal of the organized Inquisition all the governmental machinery of the Holy Roman Empire.

To gather the evidence for the conviction of suspected heretics, torture in its most exquisite and varied forms was employed to compel confession of personal guilt and betrayal of accomplices. Skilled cross-examiners were employed to use every device for drawing out damaging admissions from victims, and false promises of favor were often made to secure confession.

Handbooks of the Inquisition have preserved the means employed, not only for eliciting evidence, but the details of the whole inquisitorial process, including accusation; denunciation; examination; imprisonment in dungeons; the application of torture, with all the horrible accessories that human ingenuity could devise; the sentence, with its mocking prayer to the civil authorities for executive clemency.

Quite unlike the humanizing and refining influence of early Christianity on the barbarians, during the Inquisition, all the worst features of pagan cruelty were revived and intensified and multiplied. The entire inquisitorial procedure appealed to the basest passions of the human soul.

Hundreds of thousands of those who knew something of a more Christ-like way of life were undoubtedly destroyed, and far more were compelled by torture to deny their faith in public, then to continue, secretly, to propagate their faith. The sufferings they endured would intensify their hatred of the pretended Christianity and would furnish the impulse to spread Evangelical Christianity to every remote and inaccessible region throughout the land.

Europe became covered with a system of secret evangelical agencies that could carry forward Christian work in the very teeth of the Inquisition. Multitudes of trade guilds and secret societies became efficient and effective agencies for the propagation of evangelical teaching.

Anyone who had tasted the true spirit of the gospel of Christ could not fail to recognize the ungodly nature of the Inquisition. The Christian consciousness was outraged. The headship of the corrupted system was brought into disrepute, and there was upheaval across the continent of Europe.

Dissenting parties arose who used the apocalyptic Scriptures as a basis to predict still greater disasters and future glorious ages of righteousness and peace. There were revolts against the papacy in Germany, England, and Bohemia, and the rising contemptuous regard for the pope would be the driving force to finally bring about the Protestant Revolution of the sixteenth century.

PART III
TOWARD THE LIGHT OF THE DAWN

MEDIEVAL UNIVERSITIES

The schools of Charlemagne were the fore-runners of the great universities that were later made possible. In those early schools were taught the *trivium* and the *quadrivium* (grammar, logic, and rhetoric in the former and music, arithmetic, geometry, and astronomy in the latter).

Such schools of the early middle ages were almost confined to the monasteries, but the intellectual activity awakened by the Crusades aroused an eagerness for knowledge that became epidemic from the twelfth through the fourteenth centuries.

Some universities, such as Paris and Oxford, were developed out of monastic or cathedral schools. Others grew up around some great teacher or were founded by states or municipalities. One celebrated teacher of Roman law, whose name was Irnerius, appeared in Bologna about 1100. His reputation soon extended all over Europe, and students flocked to Bologna from all quarters. His best pupils were drawn into teaching by a growing demand due to the increased importance that came to be attached to both civil and canon (or Church) law during the eleventh and twelfth centuries.

Among all the universities established, the greatest and most influential was the University of Paris. It was fostered by popes and kings alike. The glories of the University of Paris were eloquently set forth by Lacroix:

> "If Bologna might boast her civil lawyers, Salerno her physicians, Paris might vie with these great schools in their peculiar studies, and in herself concentered the fame of all, especially of the highest - theology. The University of Paris had its inviolable privileges, its own endowments, government, laws, magistrates, jurisdiction; it was a state within a state, a city within a city, a church within a church. It refused to admit within its walls the sergeant of the mayor of Paris, the apparitors (or representatives) of the bishop of Paris; it opened its gates sullenly and reluctantly to the king's officers."

Other universities, as well, maintained a degree of freedom to teach according to their own conception of truth, and most retained the right of self-government and immunity from community interference. In case of disputes, threats to move the university to another town usually brought the municipal authorities to terms. Boycotts of obnoxious inn-keepers and shop-keepers could also keep in line the price of lodgings, provisions, writing materials, books, and other items and conditions that the university deemed necessary.

In most universities, the *trivium* and the *quadrivium* were taken over by the faculty of the arts, and typically, there were additional faculties for theology, canon and civil law, medicine, and philosophy. This four-fold division of studies was called the *Fountain of Wisdom*, and a document written in 1254 compared it to the *Four Rivers of Paradise*.

Dialectics (or logical argumentation) was highly emphasized. It was used for discussion of the subject matter between master and pupil, and masters also held public disputations among themselves, which assisted greatly toward developing the dialectic spirit.

There was, however, no such thing as research, and the use of experimentation for discovering truth was out of the question, because reason was to be held in the strictest subordination to the tenets of the Church.

The Sorbonne (a theological faculty founded by Robert Sorbon) came to be the highest theological authority in the world and frequently was in conflict with the highest church authorities.

REACTION TO ABUSE OF POWER

Most of the circumstances that worked to increase papal power eventually worked against it. The administration of Innocent III overreached itself in his claims to be "the representative of God on earth," and the irresponsible authority that he exercised by his personal power under circumstances that were favorable to him could not possibly be continued by his successors.

Frederick II, the emperor, resisted the later popes in a most determined way and called upon the princes of Europe to join him in the overthrow of the intolerable tyranny. The following paragraphs discuss the factors which led to the loss of papal prestige and power.

Though the Crusades had done much for the papacy, they had a liberalizing effect by gathering knowledge of the world beyond Europe, increasing manufacturing and trade, and causing the growth of great cities, which worked against the continuation of absolute authority.

The rigid enforcement of uniformity during the Inquisition proved so oppressive that many who had never before expressed opposition, publicly, were highly stimulated to do so. At precisely the time the Church reached the highest point of self-exaltation, opposition manifested itself almost everywhere, and soon a large proportion of the population was in open revolt.

The vast increase in the machinery of the church, brought about by the system of legates (representatives of the pope), the Crusades, the Inquisition, the wars of the popes in defense of the papal estates, the luxurious living and ever-increasing numbers in the office of the pope, all made it necessary to raise immense revenues. The need for these huge revenues, in turn, led to devising the most unscrupulous and oppressive methods of increasing revenues.

Annates, or first fruits, were exacted of bishops and abbots from the revenues of the first year of an appointment. These *Annates* could be multiplied by *Collation* from one bishpric to another. Thus a single vacancy might be made an occasion for several new appointments.

Some of the richest benefices in each country were reserved by the popes, for their own use and that of cardinals and other favorites. These *Reservations* not only represented vast revenues taken without compensation, but were often sold to the highest bidder from a number of applicants who had previously been sold *Expectancies*.

Indulgences, which had previously been given for going on crusades, were now shamelessly sold. Canon law, which had put burdensome restrictions upon almost every circumstance of life, now gave opportunity for the selling of *Dispensations* to receive forgiveness for the violation of these restrictions.

It became a leading aim with the popes to enrich their relatives to the point that *nepotism* was the universal scandal of Christendom. The enforcement of *celibacy* on the clergy and the increase in the number of monastic orders, and the membership, in the absence of any proper ethical principles, led to an appalling increase in immorality. It became widely prevalent among both clergy and monks.

The papacy became more and more the object of ambition. The cardinals restricted the choice to their own number. Bitter factions developed among them, and it became a common practice to elect the oldest and most infirm as pope, thus providing another opportunity at an early date to bring about the election of a personal favorite.

A TURN TOWARD MYSTICISM

As Christian thinking degenerated into hairsplitting subtleties and barren abstractions, those who cared more for the religious experience than for formalized statements of doctrine would have something to say about the form and ceremony of sacramentalism, which tended to destroy the immediate communion of the soul with God and failed to satisfy the deeper longings of the heart.

Toward the close of the thirteenth century, the Dominican Order that produced Thomas Aquinas, and was the chief agency in establishing and conducting the Inquisition, was the same order that in German produced a type of Mysticism, , was characterized by an intense striving to transcend the realm of humanity, and to attain the state of perfect union and communion with God.

Most of the eminent mystics were Dominican friars. It is "remarkable" that in France, Italy, and Spain, the Dominican zeal manifested itself in persecuting heretics, while in Germany it expended itself in profound contemplation of the love of God and in striving after oneness with Him.

More than one preacher of Evangelical leanings came out of the movement, but John Tauler early became a preacher of great power. In mid-career, about 1350, he came under the influence of a "Friend of God," whose identity is a mystery, and he had a profound religious experience. After years of meditation and study, he resumed his preaching in Strasbourg, where he attracted great audiences and impressed them with his impassioned eloquence. He was one of the foremost preachers of medieval times and by his sermons and writings may have done more than any other man for spreading evangelical mysticism and the promotion of spiritual Christianity.

REFORMING AND PROTESTING PARTIES

Evangelical thought undoubtedly survived through all the centuries of domination by the Church of Rome, and protests must have been made by churchmen of opposing views, from time to time, as the following example would seem to indicate.

Claudius of Turin, a bishop who died about 832, insisted on the direct relationship of the believer with God.

He denounced image worship and taught that departed saints do not wish to be worshipped and can render us no service. He declared that we are to bear the cross, not worship it. To him, crucifixes were an abomination, and pilgrimages made to holy places for merit, as well as all external works, were futile. He denied that the Apostle Peter had the power to bind, or that anyone could ever be a successor to an apostle.

The possibility of such an aggressive evangelical as Claudius being permitted to live a complete life in the episcopate of the hierarchical Church is evidence of the comparative freedom that existed at that time. His influence must have long continued in Northern Italy and Southern France, and he may be regarded as a link with the evangelicals of the twelfth century.

PETER AND HENRY

Two of the twelfth century reformers were Peter de Bruys, a priest, and Henry of Lausanne, a monk. From the little we know of Peter de Bruys, he was a pupil of Abelard, the great freethinker. For over twenty years he preached with enthusiasm and success throughout Southern France. He baptized large numbers upon their profession of faith, denounced the use of crosses, and destroyed the crosses whenever he had the opportunity. Though his preaching was considered subversive by the established order, he was able for many years to defy the hierarchy and to preserve life and liberty, but at last, about 1126, he was burned on a heap of crosses that he had lighted himself.

There is abundant testimony to the wonderful eloquence and popularity of Henry of Lausanne. In 1116 he was left in charge of the spiritual work of the diocese, by the bishop of Mans, while the bishop made a visit to

Rome. Henry already had a reputation for humility, courage, and a blameless life. The diocese records reveal that "By his speech a heart of stone could easily be moved to compunction." He soon had the diocese spiritually awakened.

The clergy and the people were moved to tears by his earnest appeals, and he is said to have resounded in such an inspirational manner that it appeared that legions of demons howled forth their disapproval each time he opened his mouth. Opposing parties complained that his wonderful manner and eloquent speech "adhered to the minds of the common people like fresh poison."

Henry is said to have associated himself with Peter de Bruys, and for ten years these zealous preachers carried on their evangelistic work together. In 1134, Henry was arrested by the archbishop of Arles and was pronounced a heretic by the Council of Pisa, but for some unknown reason was released to resume his preaching with unabated zeal.

In 1147, Pope Eugenius III commissioned Bernard of Clairvaux, the most illustrious preacher of his age, along with a cardinal, to counteract Henry's work. It was found that the people would not come near the churches and refused to pay the customary respect and reverence to the priests. Henry was finally thrown into prison, where it is likely that he died in 1148.

Peter the Venerable charged Peter and Henry with a long list of heretical views, including the denial that infants could be saved by baptism, that crosses should be adored, and that priests could offer up the body and blood of Christ. They were accused of such things as believing that sacrifices and alms for the dead were useless and that chanting is a mockery of God. Furthermore, it had been heard that Peter de Bruys rejected the authority of the Fathers and tradition, and adhered to the Scriptures alone. Peter the Venerable, in an address to the authorities in one region, wrote:

> "In your parts the people are re-baptized, the churches profaned, the altars overthrown, crosses burned; on the very day of our Lord's passion flesh is publicly eaten, priests are scourged, monks imprisoned and compelled by terrors and tortures to marry."

Then he wrote:

> "O miserable men, whoever you are who have yielded, not to many nations, but to two wretched little men only, Peter de Bruys and Henry, his pseudo-apostle."

Through the influence of Peter de Bruys and Henry of Lausanne, their followers, and other influences such as the Cathari, a gnostically inclined movement, almost the whole of Southern France had become opposed to the Roman Church by the middle of the twelfth century.

ARNOLD

Arnold, like Peter de Bruys, studied under the famous teacher and freethinker, Peter Abelard. On returning to Italy full of zeal for the reformation of both Church and State, he was admitted into one of the lower grades of the clergy. He saw, however, that the dedication of the clergy to the accumulation of wealth to be the root of the corruptions of the time, and he was able to emphasize the meaning of his scathing denunciations of ecclesiastical corruption through his own austerity and sanctity of life.

He demanded the complete renunciation of all wealth on the part of the Church, the clergy, and the monks, and a complete withdrawal from all secular affairs. He insisted that to civil rulers, alone, all property rightly belongs for its administration for the well-being of the people.

Due to a general recognition of the extreme corruption of the time, Arnold's views met with general acceptance throughout Northern Italy, but he was accused of heresy and was obliged by a synod to leave Italy. He returned to France, where he defended Abelard against Bernard of Clairvaux. He eventually had to flee to Switzerland, came back to Italy, and at last was sacrificed by treaty into the hands of Pope Alexander III.

He was hanged, and his dead body was burned. His ashes were cast into the Tiber River for fear his followers would gather his remains to be used as sacred relics.

Information about the followers of Arnold is meager, but the Arnoldists are mentioned enough in the literature of the thirteenth and fourteenth centuries to prove that they persisted as a distinct party until long after the rise of the Waldenses. Like Arnold and Peter de Bruys, the Waldenses made the church of the apostles their model, and their aim was to restore Christianity to its early purity and simplicity.

THE WALDENSES

According to some accounts, Peter Waldo, a wealthy merchant of Lyons, regularly heard Scripture in Latin, but out of curiosity, he wanted to hear it read in his own language. He employed two priests to translate from the Latin and write down large portions of the scriptures.

Apparently he was already inclined to make the Scriptures his guide, and when he understood it, he was not slow in putting it into practice. With Christ's teachings in mind to go forth, and remembering the warnings of the dangers of wealth, he distributed his means to the poor, and in about 1170, he and his disciples began teaching the Scriptures throughout the region and gained many followers.

The Archbishop of Lyons forbade them to preach on the ground that they were laymen, The Waldenses (followers of Waldo) appealed to Pope Alexander III without success in 1179, sending him some of their translated books. The pope commended their poverty, but refused to come between them and the archbishop.

They continued to teach and to preach, and appealed to Alexander's successor in 1183, again without success. In 1184, they were excommunicated at the Synod of Verona, but through their evangelical zeal, their message spread rapidly from Italy to Spain and the Rhine Valley.

As late as 1212, there were appeals by the Waldenses to Innocent III for permission to assemble for the reading of the Scriptures. It was Waldo's intention to reform the Church by teaching the Scriptures and preaching the Gospel to the common people in their own language, but it was not his choice that he and his followers be separated from the church.

According to two surviving documents of the inquisition, a convention was held in 1218 at Bergamo, Lombardy, in Italy, between the "Poor Men of Lombardy," who descended in a direct line from the Arnoldists, and the "Poor Men of Lyons," or followers of Peter Waldo.

The documents further reveal that the parties met in an endeavor to harmonize differences that had arisen between them and that both parties continued to advance toward a more truly evangelical position during the generation that followed.

One of the documents, which was designated "Passau Anonymous," mentions forty-two places in one diocese that were "infested" with the "heresy." Its teachers were described as being free from pride in the matter of attire, dressing neither luxuriously nor meanly. They were weavers and shoemakers. They avoided lying, swearing, and deceit; they were free from avarice, lived chastely, and were moderate in eating and drinking. They avoided frivolous pastimes, were always working, learning, or teaching, and committed large portions of the New Testament to memory. The writer also left a dreadful list of abuses and depraved conditions in the Church that lead to their "heretical" reaction.

The other document, the "Tractate of David of Augsburg" speaks of the Poor Men of Lyons as heretics and declared them to be more noxious than others because of their apparent simplicity and piety. It includes a routine account of their beginnings and describes them as "certain simple laymen," who in a spirit of presumption, undertook "to live absolutely according to the doctrine of the Gospel and to keep it perfectly to the letter."

An official Church document of 1308 lists ninety-two points in which the Austrian Waldenses rejected Papal doctrine and practice and held to the evangelical view. There is evidence that the party in Austria became more and more evangelical, and that they had much to do with the later evangelical movement in Bohemia and Moravia, and so with the Reformation of the sixteenth century

REFORMERS IN ENGLAND

The Hussite and Wycliffe movements were to a great extent due to the influence of older evangelical influences including the Waldenses and related parties, and they, in later years be the well-spring of movements to come.

In 1235, Robert Grossetete, a man of profound religious convictions and great learning was appointed as bishop of Lincoln. He removed unworthy priests from their positions and, as few of them could preach, he attempted to teach them how they should instruct the people, and he tried to instruct the mendicant monks on how to preach to the people..

About 1250, he wrote to the pope bewailing the corrupt state of the church, among which were the giving of special privileges to the cloisters (of monks) and the appointment of unqualified people to the clergy, with the highest offices often going to the relatives of the pope, and the giving of benefices to people who could not perform any beneficial service in return. Grossetete was regarded by most people as a saint. Heavenly music was reported to have been heard at his death and miracles to have been wrought at his tomb. His spirit was perpetuated in England until the time of Wycliffe, who quoted him as a high authority.

In 1299, Pope Boniface VII claimed that Scotland was his property. Great surprise and disgust were expressed by the nobles at the audacity of the pope. Parliament and King Edward I agreed with the nobles and ruled against the claim. In 1343, Clement VI bestowed

English benefices on two newly appointed cardinals, one of them a relative. Parliament demanded a reversal of the appointments, saying the revenues were for maintaining worship and assisting the poor in England and should not be bestowed on non-resident foreigners.

The cardinals sent agents to collect their revenues, but were driven away in disgrace. The pope appealed to the king, but Edward I wrote with great boldness and severity against the unrighteousness of the papal proceedings. Edward II allowed the pope to regain his power in England, but under Edward III, statutes were enacted by Parliament that set forth at great length the great evils that England had suffered from the bestowment of benefices upon unworthy men and foreigners who had performed no service for the English people.

WYCLIFFE

After some Englishmen had been called before the pope to account for church property, a law was passed that made it a crime against the State to arraign any subject of England before a foreign tribunal. By the time of Wycliffe, around 1320, there was widespread opposition to the usurpations of the papacy.

Wycliffe, like other church reformers before him, had from early in life, strong convictions with regard to the unity of the church. The belief was that as the church is one, so it ought to have a single head.

The papal schism (when there were two rival popes) in 1378 made a deep impression on him, and from that time forth he declared that it would be better for the church of Christ if both popes were removed from office. For that reason, and for the corruption, he began to look upon the pope as an antichrist and to see in the papacy the fulfillment of the apocalyptic prophesies. He also declared that only two orders of ministry were established by Christ, presbyters and deacons, and that the introduction of other orders was not in the true spirit of Christianity.

The aspects of the papacy that most offended Wycliffe were the extortion of funds from England, the robbing of the poor, the appointment of foreigners who would not minister to the people, benefices, and the sending forth of mendicant monks, who begged, not for the supplying of their wants, but for enriching the monasteries, and who used all sorts of methods for extorting money from the rich and poor.

Wycliffe wrote, among many other works, numerous popular treatises to counteract the influence of the monks, who were at this time gaining predominance in the University of Oxford. He appointed what he called *poor priests* to evangelize and distribute these materials throughout England. These missionaries met with great acceptance wherever they went.

In 1381, the chancellor of the University condemned Wycliffe when he began to discredit the doctrine of transubstantiation, and prohibited him from speaking again on that doctrine. About the same time, there was an insurrection of the peasants, which was attributed to Wycliffe's doctrines being spread by the *poor priests*. The archbishop of Canterbury condemned a series of Wycliffe's writings as heretical, and was a cause of his leaving Oxford. The rest of his life was spent in writing and preaching. He published his English translation of the Bible in 1380.

Forty-four years after his death in 1384, it was ordered that his bones be removed from consecrated ground, after which, they were burned and thrown into a river.

THE LOLLARDS

The circulation of Wycliffe's popular evangelical writings, his English translation of the Bible, and the evangelizing activity of his *Poor Priests* awakened the remnants of the evangelicals that still remained from the early British and Iro-Scottish form of Christianity.

These influences multiplied immensely the number of people on the British Isles who would recognize no other authority in religion than the Word of God. A new party, known as the Lollards, came into being and, like Wycliffe, was favored by a number of powerful nobles, but unlike Wycliffe, those of the new party were not hampered by such beliefs as the *reality of the one universal church* and did not hesitate to separate themselves totally from the Church.

In 1395 the Lollards presented a memorial (or declaration) to Parliament which declared, in part, that corruption in the Church was caused by pride and that the priesthood which began in Rome is not the priesthood that Christ ordained. The memorial condemned the law of celibacy, the doctrine of transubstantiation, prayers for the dead, and auricular confession, and explained that these laws cause unnatural vice, witchcraft, and idolatry, and that they exalt the pride of the priests and provide them the opportunity to use secret conversations for vicious and self-serving purposes. The memorial reveals the boldness and zeal of the party and their spirit of reform, which was a return to primitive simplicity and purity of doctrine and life.

Due to the fact that the Inquisition had never been fully established in England, historical documents on the subject of British evangelicals are rather scarce, but up to the time of the memorial of the Lollards to the Parliament, no adequate measures had been adopted by the Roman Church for the suppression of the reforming party.

With the accession of Thomas Arundel, as Archbishop of Canterbury, and the crowning of Henry IV as king, an act was passed for the arrest, trial, and the burning of the Lollards. All unauthorized meetings, schools, books, and all unauthorized teaching and preaching were to be suppressed, and the Inquisition, which had not previously been effective on the British Isles, was now pushed forward with great vigor. Many Lollards were burned, and the party was driven into secrecy. From time to time they were discovered, and others lost their lives, yet they persisted in considerable numbers until the Reformation.

JOHN HUSS IN BOHEMIA

Bohemia first received the gospel in the ninth century from the Greek Church, then, gradually became acquainted with the Latin forms of the Church, but up to the time of John Huss, the Bohemians were always glad to hear from those who opposed the pretensions of Rome.

Under Charles IV (1346-1378), Bohemia was brought fully under papal control. Prague was made an archbishopric (the seat of an archbishop), magnificent cathedrals were built, and the most vigorous laws against heretics were enacted. The University of Prague was established for the propagation of papal doctrine throughout Bohemia and Moravia.

Such triumphant moments for the Church were followed by almost immediate rejection. The enrichment of the churches led to such decay in the morals of the clergy that it became a major cause in a demand for reform, and the university became an instrument of opposition to the papacy.

The Archbishop of Prague was a man of great purity of life. He was earnest in his efforts to reform the clergy and was supported in these efforts by Emperor Charles IV. During their tenure in office, conditions were right for the appearance of a number of eloquent and zealous evangelical preachers who prepared the way for the reforming work of John Huss. One of the evangelists was Conrad of Waldhausen, who was called to Prague around 1360.

Conrad, an Austrian, and an Augustinian monk, had gained a high reputation for eloquence at Vienna and was full of zeal in preaching the gospel of repentance. The people flocked to hear him, but he aroused the animosity of the monks and the clergy. They made accusations against him, but did not appear on the appointed day of his trial. Conrad's work was effective, even though he only spoke in German and Latin.

Before Conrad's death, a native Bohemian of greater genius would appear. Militsch of Kremster, private secretary to Charles IV, who already held a high ecclesiastical position and had observed the extreme corruption of the Church, renounced his dignities and income in 1363, adopted an ascetic mode of life, and resolved in humility and poverty to follow Christ in preaching the gospel.

It was a new thing when he began to preach in the Bohemian language and the people were able to hear the gospel in their native tongue. In a short time his ministry was thronged so that every day he preached two or three hours at a time, and he preached several times on Sundays and fast days. Little Venice, an ill-famed part of town, was destroyed at his direction, and in its place was built a house of refuge, called Little Jerusalem, for more than 200 women who had been induced to abandoned their former way of life.

In a study of the apocalyptic Scriptures, Militsch became convinced that Antichrist had come in the corruption of the church. In 1367 he went to Rome to inform the pope of the new light he had received, and in the absence of the pope, he published his views on the door of St. Peter's. For this, he was arrested and imprisoned until the pope returned. After his release, he was discouraged, but soon returned to his former work with new zeal and began to train new evangelists. In 1374, after accusations of heresy against him had been made by the monks, he journeyed to Avignon to vindicate his orthodoxy. There, he fell sick, and died.

Matthias of Janow, the son of a Bohemian knight, had spent six years in the University of Paris as a student of philosophy and theology. He had traveled much in Germany and Italy, and was one of the most cultivated men of the time. He said that during his early school life he had been a slave of his passions, but there "entered into his breast a certain fire, subtle, new, strong, and unusual, but exceedingly sweet."

The papal schism had already occurred when Matthias entered into his work, at which time two or three rival popes were demanding the allegiance of the people and anathematizing one another. He was therefore motivated more definitely than Militsch to center his notions of Antichrist upon the papacy and wrote that the papal schism came about "not because they loved Jesus Christ and his church, but because they loved themselves and this world."

He combated the notion that the clergy are the church and the notion that ordinary Christians should not be often admitted to the elements of the Supper, which he regarded as a most important means of grace. He strongly emphasized the universal priesthood of believers, one of the burning issues of the Bohemian revolution.

The writings of Wycliffe had been introduced into the University of Prague after the marriage of Anne, daughter of Charles IV to Richard II of England in 1382, when considerable correspondence had been established between Oxford and the University of Prague. By the time John Huss appeared on the scene, Wycliffe's writings were held in high esteem and were a very great influence on him.

John Huss was born in 1367 and was educated at the University of Prague, where he became bachelor in 1393 and master in 1396. He rapidly advanced and became rector of the university in 1403. Up until 1402, when he was appointed preacher in the Bethlehem Chapel, established under the influence of Militsch, he had taken more interest in philosophy and scholastic theology than in evangelical work.

He studied the philosophical writings of Wycliffe and used them in his lectures. Through these studies, he adopted Wycliffe's *realistic* philosophy. His duty as preacher to the people and his sense of responsibility led him to study the Scriptures as he had never done before, and he came to feel that the great evils in the Church had resulted largely from neglect of biblical study.

About the same time he became acquainted with Wycliffe's theological works through Jerome of Prague, who had studied at Oxford. Under the inspiration of his intense study of the bible and the works of Wycliffe, Huss soon won a great reputation as a moral preacher and in 1405 began to denounce the corruption of the clergy and in this he received the support of King

Waclav. By preaching against the clergy, he made many enemies, and his Bohemian patriotism and zeal in defending and widely spreading the views of Wycliffe made him odious to the Germans in the university. In this he stirred up so much controversy that the university forbade him to discuss them.

Miracles were supposed to be regularly taking place by the pretended blood of Christ in the church at Wilsnack. Huss was appointed to a commission to visit the place and investigate the matter. A fraud was exposed, and pilgrimages to Wilsnack were forbidden.

In 1409, due to the nationalistic aversion of the Bohemians, the Germans lost many of their privileges in the university and withdrew from Bohemia. Huss was now completely dominant at the university. The archbishop had become jealous of his influence and felt rebuked by his denunciations of the clergy. In 1410 the archbishop procured a bull (or edict) from Pope Alexander V that forbade preaching in private chapels and required the burning of Wycliffe's works.

Huss, under the support of the king and queen, the nobility, and the university, continued preaching in the chapel and defending Wycliffe's works. After a time, the archbishop was compelled to withdraw his order and accusation of heresy.

In 1412 the pope issued a bull for crusades against Waclav with the usual promise of indulgences. Huss, and his friend, Jerome, from Oxford, now protested with greater zeal than before against the abuses. This led to the condemnation of Wycliffe's works by the Church and to the excommunication of Huss in 1413.

Huss retired from Prague and wrote his great work on the church. He was summoned to appear before the council of Constance in 1414 and went under the safe-conduct of Emperor Sigismund. He felt secure from the fact that he had not been charged with heresy and that the object of the council was reformation.

Safety for Huss was only an illusion. Emperor Sigismund, who called the council, was no friend of the Bohemians. The preponderance of power on the council was German, and it was remembered that Huss had been chiefly instrumental in driving away the Germans from Prague. As the council met without papal summons, they could not afford to appear sympathetic with revolutionary spirits or appear to be a failure. It was clear that if Huss were allowed to return to Bohemia, he would, without fail, carry on a revolution which would result in the alienation of Bohemia from the Church.

On November 28, he was thrown into prison on the charge of heresy, and despite protests from the University of Prague and the Bohemian nobles, the safe-conduct of the emperor was violated, and without the show of a fair trial, Huss was burned in July of 1415.

The martyrdom of John Huss set off the great civil wars in Bohemia, known as the Hussite Wars and later inspired Martin Luther in his revolt against the Church.

BRETHREN OF THE COMMON LIFE

The Brethren of the Common Life originated in the Netherlands as a result of the evangelical mysticism of Johann Ruysbroek. Gerhard Groot and Florentius, a convert, combined the most evangelical type of mysticism with semi-monastic life and enthusiastic devotion to evangelistic work, education, and literary production. With the permission of his bishop and under the advice of the aged Ruysbroek, Groot began preaching repentance and conversion to multitudes of eager listeners around 1379. A number of well-educated evangelical men were soon at his side, ready to carry forward the work.

Groot did not intend to break with the church and he hesitated to adopt the communal system, fearing opposition of the monks, but he was persuaded by Florenius to make the experiment and leave the results to God.

The peculiarity of their organization consisted in voluntary association based on devout living and work, such as copying books, which would be done for their support. They did away with the use of vows and did not allow begging. They engaged in teaching and preaching as time allowed, preaching justification by faith, and they were careful to insist on the necessity of upright and devout living.

John Pupper of Goch and several other important evangelists arose under the influence of the Brethren of the Common Life in the last century before the reformation. He emphasized the authority of the Scriptures, rightly interpreted, and was against traditionalism and ecclesiastical authority.

He stressed that love to God and man embodies the essence of religion. He rejected the speculations of scholasticism as vain and useless and denied that reason could penetrate the realms of the supernatural.

Only by the "light of faith and of grace," he believed, can one apprehend the "supremely true" and the "supremely good." He preached justification by faith and repudiated the whole mediaeval system of justification by works, regarding saving faith as a transforming process, wherein the believer is not only declared righteous, but is made righteous in truth.

OTHER OLD EVANGELICALS

In Bohemia and Moravia there were hundreds of congregations of Bohemian Brethren. Along with their many thousands of members, there were many unattached supporters from the gentry and nobility. They had good schools and good literature. From the time the printing press was invented, they had taken better advantage of its use than any other group.

Among other groups, the Brethren of the Common Life, who arose in the Netherlands in the fourteenth century, spread into most parts of Germany, established schools, and devoted their attention to the study of the Scriptures and to the attainment of inner piety.
They insisted that whomsoever God will save, He will save by his grace.

CONSIDERATIONS FAVORING REFORM

ECONOMIC AND SOCIAL CONDITIONS

Germany was a part of the Holy Roman Empire, but it was still in a thoroughly feudalized and disintegrated condition. By virtue of the German law of inheritance, the land had been endlessly subdivided among the sons of the lords, and in only a few cases were there any large territories of great political power.

Many petty principalities were interspersed with ecclesiastical estates, all governed in very much the same way, and all claiming and exercising the right of private warfare. The more important principalities were both able and inclined to resist any interference with their internal affairs, leaving the emperor with little control in most parts of Germany.

The development of the mineral resources of Saxony and adjoining provinces led the papal office to adopt means of raising money that amounted to extortion, and because of such practices, the Germans came to look upon the papacy as a foreign and corrupt power interested in Germany only for exploitation. Such a condition strongly added to the ability of reformers to raise widespread protests against the practices of the Church.

Increased wealth brought about an increased demand for manufactured goods, which in turn, brought about a tremendous growth of the cities. Some cities were able, for the first time, to emancipate themselves from their feudal lords and obtain imperial charters as free cities.

These cities governed themselves and were represented in the emperor's diet (or assembly) side by side with the electors and princes of the states (although any decisions made in the emperor's diet were usually ignored). In many of the free cities a spirit of toleration prevailed that enabled the older forms of evangelical Christianity to flourish, even when persecution prevailed in other places.

The growth of the cities brought in many artisans who organized themselves into guilds, which from the early Middle Ages were found by Christians to be important as a means of evangelical propagation. The formation and spread of secret societies of every sort is most characteristic of the time. Most, without doubt, were intended for the spread of the *New Learning*, and some, in reality, were actually evangelical churches, intended for the spread of the gospel.

France had become a mighty and thoroughly centralized monarchy. One by one the old feudal provinces were brought under the dominion of the state. In 1516, Francis I had entered into an agreement with the pope that the king was to nominate the prelates (high church officials) in France, and the pope and the king would share the advantages of patronage to the institutions of the Church. This understanding, there is little doubt, was a reason that the pope supported the king in his bid for the imperial crown in 1519 that resulted in great injury to the papal cause in Germany.

France was a mighty power, second only to Spain, but she had ambitions of being the mightiest of all. She was not content with any permanent eastern boundary and was not interested in contributing to the power of the Empire, but if France had supported the emperor during the early years of the Protestant Revolution, it is difficult to see how the Protestant princes of Germany could have protected the reforming movements in their provinces.

Spain was approaching the height of its glory. Its king was emperor; the Moors and the Jews had been excluded; its territories were being united; and the discovery and exploitation of America and the East were adding to its riches.

A ferocious type of Roman Catholicism had been developed, partly as a result of contact and conflict with Mohammedanism that brought on the Order of the Jesuits, the enforced conversion of heathen people, the Inquisition, and the uncompromising warfare with Protestantism.

The ambitions of Spain were boundless, but her schemes were fortunately held in check by similar ambitions on the part of France. The attention of the emperor was also distracted by the aggressive attitude of the

Turks toward much of the imperial territory in the eastern provinces of Germany. These distractions were a great advantage to the Protestants as they revolted in large parts of Germany against the Roman ecclesiastical system.

THE RISE OF NEW LEARNING

From the time of Charlemagne, there was considerable literary activity in the monasteries, but it was not directed toward learning. Under the influence of dead formalism, and aimless hairsplitting there was little effort or inclination among medieval theologians to arrive at new views of truth.

The Latin text of the Bible was regarded as infallibly correct, and the Church had determined how it was to be interpreted. There was, therefore, no reason for the medieval theologians to turn to the Scriptures for the truth. Because of these conditions, Medieval theology would furnish one of the strongest barriers to progress toward true enlightenment, but, it would in the end, yield to the steady march of truth.

The continued encroachment of the Turks upon the Greek Empire, and finally, the fall of Constantinople in 1453 caused a large number of Greek scholars to take refuge in Italy. There they were welcomed, and their services as teachers of the Greek language and philosophy were in great demand. In 1450, a school was founded by Cosmo de' Medici for the promotion of classical studies.

In the study of Plato, it was shown that scholastic theology, in comparison with Platonic philosophy, had much to be desired. It was also shown that the scholastic schoolmen had not properly understood Aristotle, whom they professed to follow.

The study of antiquity became a passion. Monastic libraries were ransacked by those seeking reference to the Greek and Roman classics. The study of Greek became the fashion of the day, and to write like Cicero became the obsession. The invention of the printing press around that time was a powerful asset to the new learning. Popes and civil rulers, alike, were lavish in their expenditures on literature, architecture, and the fine arts.

A taste of the elegant literature of Greece and Rome took their minds off scholastic theology. The high ideals of Platonism were considered by many to be more divine than the stiff formalism of Thomas Aquinas. This lead many to deny any superiority of the Christian religion over paganism, but the attempts to harmonize Christianity with Platonism led to the study of the writings of both in their original languages. Thus, the study of the Bible in Greek and Hebrew was revived, and made possible its better understanding.

The spirit of the Renaissance pervaded the religious, social, and political life of the time. The office of the pope, itself, came under its spell, and several of the popes were more devoted to literature and art than to the interests of religion and the maintaining of ecclesiastical power. Educational methods were revolutionized. Theology experienced a new birth, and philosophy was transformed by the giants of the new learning.

The principle of freedom from authority in matters of thought and worship began to be developed, but was not fully grasped. While reformers claimed freedom for themselves, no one considered freedom for those of opposing views until a much later time. The first signs of the modern spirit of freedom arose from humanitarian concerns rather than from the inspiration of their religious thinking.

HUMANISTIC REFORMERS

In the latter part of the fifteenth century, a number of able scholars reappeared England and other countries north of the Alps to devote their lives to the advancement of learning. Some had studied in Italy, where they became exceptional Greek scholars and were immersed in the spirit of the Renaissance.

Colet was one of such men. He was a man of genius, and brought a deep and spiritual insight to his study of the languages and soon came to the conclusion that the Bible, interpreted in harmony with known history and known usage of the original languages, rather than by the allegorical method of the schoolmen, is the only true source of religious knowledge.

His lectures on the epistles of Paul first astonished, then delighted and inspired the crowds of students and doctors who attended. At a convocation in 1512, as dean of St. Paul's Cathedral in London, he preached a strong reformatory sermon to churchmen from all over England bewailing the pride, greed, and self-indulgence of the clergy. No one of his time showed more profound insight into Christian truth.

Erasmus came under the influence of Colet in 1498. His father and mother had provided for his education in the famous school of the Brethren of the Common Life at Deventer, but the dishonesty of the trustee of his funds brought an end to his studies. He was placed in a monastic school in 1481, at the age of sixteen, where he "as good as wasted" three years. Destitute of means, he entered a monastery to take up a way life which he undoubtedly abhorred, but in 1493 was permitted by the bishop to go to Paris for the continuance of his studies.

At some point during his studies, he had become convinced that theological study would lead him to heresy, and he said that he "had not the courage to become a heretic." He dropped out, then later, returned to Paris, where he became Bachelor of Theology in 1498, but his dislike for scholastic theology was profound.

His association with Colet and other humanists of England stimulated him to undertake the mastery of Greek and to enter upon his distinguished literary career. Early success assured the support he needed for his long-cherished dream, which was to study in Italy.

When Erasmus returned to Germany, he resumed a writing career of astonishing success. The rapid publication of both his popular and learned works gave him a position of honor in the literary world beyond anything his age had known.

His occasional journeys through Germany were like triumphal processions, and large numbers of young scholars caught their inspiration from him. He wrote a satire, "Praise of Folly," in which he ridiculed and repudiated monkish and papal views of piety, and then proclaimed the true principles of Christianity. Among his many other works was a critical edition of the Greek New Testament, in which he included as a preface a noble appeal to all those who had lost faith in Christianity.

Through the great popularity of his writings, he was able to scatter his reformatory views far and wide. To scholastic theologians, he spoke of the folly of paying more attention to the writings of medieval theologians than to the plain and simple words of Christ and His apostles. Most leaders of the Reformation owed their knowledge of the Scriptures to Erasmus.

THE REFORMING FORCES AT WORK

The Roman Church and its hierarchy had benefited Europe as a civilizing and stabilizing force on society, but it had become hopelessly corrupt and all efforts to reform it from within had apparently ended in dismal failure.

Evangelical influences of many types had long been powerfully at work and capable of enduring all the fiery tests that could be brought down upon them, but they were scattered, and in some regions, almost exterminated.

As a result of contemptuous and cruel triumph over a long history of protests, the pretended representatives of true Christianity went on to become more arrogant and unscrupulous. Men, such as Wycliffe and Huss, in a number of states of Europe, rose up and cried out against the extortion and oppression to which their fatherlands had been subjected by a foreign and unfriendly hierarchy. These movements were met with a hearty and patriotic response from all classes of society, but were not destined to be a lasting success.

Such patriotic movements offered stout resistance to the tyranny for the time, but were soon swept away in the tide of corruption which their efforts were not adequate to prevent. The fact that the reformers continued to maintain a belief in the *reality* of the *one universal church,* conceived to be that for which all else existed, was detrimental to a Biblical basis for the church and assured that reform could only be a fleeting notion.

The mystics, though holding to many extravagant notions, reintroduced the concept of an inner life, and believing in the insufficiency of outward forms, recognized the need for a personal relationship of man with God. Through the sanctity of their inner lives and through the profound conviction of sin and grace that were set forth in their literature and sermons, they did much to awaken religious interest, but mysticism was indifferent to the church as an institution and could not of itself bring about a radical reform.

The Revival of Learning was absolutely essential to the Reformation. It awakened freedom of thought and undermined the principle of the divine right of any human authority, and it undermined the scholastic concepts that had caused many, in disgust, to lose faith in Christianity, itself.

Many turned to pagan literature and began to study Greek, some to become devotees to Neo-Platonism, and others, ironically, to study the .Scriptures in the original languages, free from the influence of traditional interpretations.

The knowledge and understanding that the Revival of Learning brought forth could not alone bring about a religious reform, but it was indispensable among the forces required to shake the religion of Europe to its foundations and bring an end to the long, dark night.

PART IV
REVOLUTION AND REFORM
THE PROTESTANT REVOLUTION

PREPARING MARTIN LUTHER

Born about 1483, of hard working and deeply religious peasants, Martin Luther's early life was embittered by poverty and harsh treatment at home that drove him at last into a convent. His father, a miner, was ambitious for him and provided him with the best education within his reach. Martin advanced rapidly and could read Latin at a very early age.

While pursuing his studies at Magdeburg and Eisenach, he partly supported himself by singing from door to door. In 1501, he entered the University of Erfurt, where he not only pursued the ordinary studies of the medieval curriculum, but also had contact with the New Learning, and was introduced, as well, to Augustine and the German mystics by the devout and learned Johann von Staupitz.

Luther advanced to the Bachelor of Arts in 1502, the Master of Arts in 1505, then, in the summer of the same year assumed monastic vows as a member of the Augustinian convent at Erfurt.

Staupitz was an evangelically disposed official of the Augustinian Order, who was able at a critical period in Luther's experience to give him the spiritual guidance away from superstitious dependence on dead works as a means of salvation and toward the acceptance of a message that made him a free man in Christ.

Staupitz had become a member of the Augustinian Order at a very young age. The order laid much stress on the study of the Scriptures and on the writings of Augustine, the great theological thinker of the fourth and fifth centuries. Under the influence of the New Learning and of evangelical mysticism, many of the members of the order had already developed a strong
dislike for the dry and barren scholastic theology that still held sway in the universities.

In 1497 Staupitz was already Master of Arts. In 1498 he became Biblical Bachelor, a degree attained by completing several years of Bible study. By 1500 he received the Doctor of Theology degree. By this time he had become greatly distinguished for learning, religious zeal, and administrative ability, and his services as a teacher and as an official in the monastic order were in great demand. He was, also, much sought after by the wealthy and intellectually blessed among the nobility, and he was a profound influence upon them.

From 1502 onward, Staupitz aided Frederick the Wise in establishing the University of Wittenberg and became Dean of the Theological Faculty as well as Professor of Theology. To create a university with the image of the earnest and spiritually minded Staupitz pressed upon it speaks well of Frederick's motives as
he directed much of the wealth of Saxony to Christian education.

Evangelical Augustinianism became the dominant influence from the beginning, and Staupitz stayed abreast of the tide of evangelical thought sweeping through Germany. The best expression of those evangelical thoughts can be found in the sermons of Tauler, a

German mystic of the fourteenth century and a little book entitled *German Theology*, which had become a famous handbook among the spiritually minded evangelicals. Through these studies Staupitz had become convinced that religion is not a matter of form and ceremony, but of direct communion between the individual soul and God, and that salvation is not gained by outward works, but by an inward process that transforms the character.

In 1505, Staupitz, as an official of the Augustinian Order, visited the monastery at Erfurt. His attention was called to the gifted, young Martin Luther, who was in sore distress and was vainly striving, by bodily mortification and ritualistic observances, to pacify his troubled soul. Staupitz's earnest and spiritual words to him were "as a voice from heaven." He taught Luther to look upon God as a God of love, who not only sought the salvation of fallen man, but who made an infinite sacrifice to that end.

In 1508, Luther, already a Master of Arts at the University of Erfurt, was transferred, through the intervention of Staupitz, to the Augustinian monastery at Wittenberg. There, he soon became Biblical Bachelor, and later, Doctor of Theology.

It was on behalf of Staupitz that Luther visited Rome in 1510 to 1511, where he became intimately acquainted with the heathenish life in the papal court. Luxury and license were everywhere in evidence. He now realized, as never before, the uses that were being made of the vast sums of money that were being extorted, year after year, from the German people, and he witnessed the contempt in which these same German people were held by the courtly Italians.

Luther entered upon his work as professor at Wittenberg, aware of the corrupt state of the Church and earnestly desiring both ecclesiastical reform and the relief of the unjust burdens being heaped upon his people. Soon afterward, Staupitz left the university to spread his evangelical principles to the monasteries from Germany to Austria and the Netherlands, and among the circles of enlightened evangelical men. There, Staupitz was looked upon as "the very tongue of Paul" and considered him to be "the one who should free Israel."

Luther was in full accord with the spirit of evangelism expressed by Staupitz and expressed this in his own published works during the years following 1515. In 1516 he wrote an enthusiastic preface to the anonymous work, *German Theology,* which was so well received as to have ten editions in rapid order.

When, in 1517, Luther posted his Ninety-five Theses on the door of the church in Whittenburg, he quickly had the enthusiastic support, not only of Staupitz, but all of his Nuremberg friends, and of evangelicals everywhere. Many who had expressed evangelical views only in secret, now declared them openly.

As a sign that Luther had surpassed Staupitz in his influence over the German people and become the standard-bearer of the older evangelical type of religious life and thought, one of the Nuremberg friends greeted him as the one raised up of God to lead the people of Israel out of their captivity.

THE LUTHERAN REFORMATION

After posting his theses against the sale of indulgences in 1517, which placed him under the censure of the Church, Luther proceeded to publish a number of polemical tracts on indulgences, monastic vows, and other subjects. These endeavors gained him the enthusiastic support of evangelicals and mystics everywhere, and he stood as the champion of Christian liberty and equality until about-1520.

In 1517 he wrote on the subject, "Liberty of a Christian Man." As late as 1523, he wrote, warning the princes that the times have changed and that unless they rule justly, God will put an end to their authority, and he warned them that God will not suffer them to rule the souls of men, for in so doing they are sure to bring upon themselves the hatred of God and of men.

His doctrinal views during those times appeared to be almost identical to those of the old evangelical Christianity, with which the peasants of Germany had long been familiar. Even as late as 1524, in a letter to the princes of Saxony, he wrote: "Your princely graces" should not restrain the preaching of the word and should allow men to preach "what they can and against whom they will...." Luther's words were truly brave, but living up to those words was another matter.

Staupitz, who was long Luther's teacher, friend, and spiritual counselor, had already begun to sense a drift in Luther's stand in his publications. By 1522 Luther had drifted so far from Staupitz as to be able to write:

> "Staupitz's letters I do not understand, except that I see that they are very empty in spirit; besides, he does not write to me as he used to do. May God bring him back."

There is no evidence that Staupitz had changed in the slightest degree in his attitude toward truth. It was Luther that was changing, and with childlike simplicity, he seemed to believe that it was Staupitz who was drifting away.

While Luther had railed against indulgences, monastic vows and other abuses, he had placed himself outside the good will of both the pope and the Emperor. The practical, political, and militant side of the work in which he was engaged, no doubt, tended to eliminate thinking in the gentle terms of the mystics and the old evangelical Christianity and to replace it with harsher modes of thought and expression.

Luther, apparently, had decided that the only way to withstand the combined wrath of the papal and imperial powers was by satisfying the wishes of the German princes, whose armed support he deemed indispensable.

He is by common consent the central figure of the Protestant Revolution. His powerful personality gave shape and direction to the movement that came to be called by his name. He railed against the papacy, but because of his *realistic* view of the *universal church,* as taught by the *Scholastics*, he would have been shocked at the very suggestion of schism (or breaking away from the Church). He believed that the Church could be reformed, but he compromised the true spirit of Christianity as he held to the belief that religion is a matter to be enforced by law.

Both he and the direction of the movement which he led were filled with many inconsistencies, and the results of his reform fell short of all that was hoped could be attained. He railed against the papacy for all the abuses against the German people, yet he wrote:

> "If the pope really knew what was going on, he would rather see St. Peter's Church go up in ashes than to see it built from the skin and bones of his sheep."

The most conspicuous of Luther's inconsistencies had to do with his earlier evangelical views on the one hand and his condemnation of the peasants for their uprising on the other hand. His bold statements against the Church incited a widespread uprising against tyranny, yet, as he raged against them, he became more than a willing bystander to their massacre.

CHARGED AND CONDEMNED

Luther was ordered to appear at Rome to be examined, but Frederick the Wise, arranged for him to be examined at Augsburg by Cardinal Legate (or representative) Cajetan in October, 1518.

Neither kindness nor threats availed anything with Luther. Cajetan wrote to Frederick, giving him an account of Luther's conduct and asking him to send him to Rome or banish him from the realm. Luther also wrote to give his view of the conference. Cajetan charged Luther with rejecting a decree of a pope with regard to indulgences. Luther answered that the decree was clearly opposed to the meaning of the Scripture upon which it was supposedly based.

The attitude of Cajetan in the conference was that of a superior who would not stoop to argue with a miserable monk. He demanded of Luther unconditional submission and warned him to be concerned for the salvation of his soul. Frederick refused to banish Luther, but considered his arraignment before an impartial tribunal in Germany to be a reasonable demand.

Luther was summoned to yet other conferences and was involved in disputes on theology and the corrupt administration of the Church. He wrote constantly and feverishly on such subjects as his plan for reform and the hopelessness of reform in the established Church.

A bull (or papal order) of Luther's excommunication was issued in June, 1520, and he was summoned, with a promise of safe-conduct, to a diet to meet at Worms (in the Rhineland) in January, 1521. As was completely expected, he refused to recant (reverse his opinion) or discredit himself with his large and enthusiastic following, and as expected, the diet condemned his radical views.

The representatives of Rome insisted that no faith be kept with heretics and that Luther should be executed forthwith, but the young and newly crowned emperor refused to take lightly the promise of safe-conduct and permitted him to leave Worms unmolested. Luther was seized by friends in disguise and taken to Wartburg Castle, near Eisenach, for protection.

According to the Edict of Worms, all of Luther's books were to be burned, and prohibitions were placed on their circulation, but the people and the princes of the territories who favored Luther usually ignored the edict.

LUTHER'S LATER YEARS

A war broke out between the emperor and France in the same year of the Edict of Worms, which was a great advantage to the Protestant cause and the protection of Luther. The emperor's forces were diverted for many years, not only by the war with France, but by his invasion of Italy and threats of a Turkish invasion. Consequently, Luther was left free much of the time to rail against the pope and to condemn all other reforming efforts.

Because of Luther's turbulent and impulsive nature, he came to feel that his knowledge, alone, was the knowledge of the truth, that his cause was the cause of God, and those who opposed him were undoubtedly opponents of God. He spent his life trying to tear down papal authority, but he presumed virtually the same authority, himself, as he regarded himself the great representative of God's cause on earth. Because other reforming movements were not in complete agreement with his own, he considered them as tools of Satan. His movement speedily became as openly intolerant and atrocious in its persecuting measures as was the Roman system, itself.

His writings abound in lamentations over the condition of the churches and his contempt for the clergy. He decried the increased use of spirits and brandy, while indulging in wine and beer drinking without restraint and trusting "that the Lord God would excuse him for occasional excesses." He insisted that each Christian should believe himself to be holy and should glory in his holiness, however sinful his life might be. Otherwise, he said, one does not place enough faith in the Christ who died for his sins.

Luther's intemperance in speech and drink, and his intolerance of opposition, left the Lutheran countries without the positive influence they needed to turn back the tide of immorality and hostility toward religion. In 1546, Luther died a natural death, perhaps hastened by his own excesses.

A MODERATING SPIRIT

Philip Melanchthon, a thorough-going humanist and one of the most accomplished classical scholars of the time, became Luther's closest advisor. He was far more moderate than Luther and worked to curb the raw and inflammatory language that was usual in Luther's correspondence.

Melanchthon continued to be a moderating force throughout the great controversies that affected the development of Lutheranism. He wrote *the Augsburg Confession*[56] in that same moderating spirit for the bene-

---

[56]See "The Augsburg Confession," A.D. 1530. Reproduced by

fit of the emperor, who had invited protesting parties to the Diet for the presentation of explicit statements of their tenets.

Melanchthon's aim was to minimize the differences between Lutheran and Catholic doctrine and to use language so ambiguous on crucial points that it could be interpreted in a Catholic sense without contradicting Lutheran teaching. At the same time, he took great pains to separate Lutheranism from the beliefs of the Zwinglians and Anabaptists. The *Augsburg Confession* became the first and most important definition of Lutheranism..[57]

THE ZWINGLIAN REFORMATION

The preaching of Zwingli was far more wholesome in its influence than was Luther's. Although he preached justification by faith, as Luther did, he did not leave the impression that good works were not worth performing, and the Zwinglian Reformation was much more emotionally controlled. No one spoke with such anger as Luther. Contempt for Rome was taken for granted in Switzerland, and preaching against abuses excited little astonishment. While the Zwinglian Reformation caused less uproar, it promised to be more far-reaching, due to the fact that Zwingli, unlike Luther, came to be convinced that a break from the Roman Church would be necessary.

Zwingli, about 1506, as a pastor still receiving subsistence from the pope, began to devote a great part of his time to the study of Latin classics and philosophy, and he preached eloquently in favor of reform.

From 1513 he regarded his study of the Greek New Testament as one of the most important steps in his

---

Schaff, Vol. III, 3
[57]Schaff, I, 221-222.

preparation as a reformer. New light seemed to dawn upon the sacred Word, and the influence of Erasmus, who took up residence in Basel, was greatly important to his development. Through his Biblical studies, he saw the need of reform, both in his own life and the population in general.

About 1516 he began preaching simple sermons to explain the Scriptures, and in 1518 became chief preacher in Zurich. He abandoned the customary mode of preaching from texts arranged by the authorities and began expounding entire books of the Bible in regular order.

This method was very popular and practical, and his messages were directed against superstition, hypocrisy, idleness, and excessive eating and drinking, while calling for changes toward consistent Christian living. He urged rulers to be just, to protect widows and orphans, and to maintain the independence of the Swiss confederacy as a bulwark against oppression.

In 1520, the Council of Zurich authorized that henceforth all preachers should preach freely from the Old and New Testaments, but it barred them from discussing changes from customary doctrine and practice. It was a decision made against Zwingli, but Zwingli was agreeable, as he cared only for liberty to expound the Scriptures. He felt that abuses would vanish if true doctrine were preached and if true understanding of the Scriptures were realized. (Obvious influence of Erasmus).

Zwingli was highly patriotic and protective of the welfare of Swiss citizens against the papacy. After giving up his papal subsistence in 1520, he strongly denounced the mercenary system which provided Swiss soldiers to fight the wars of the popes. In 1522 he wrote a paper, "On Choice and Freedom in Eating," after defending certain Zurich citizens who had been thrown into prison for eating meat on a fast day.

Zwingli also wrote an exhortation against clerical celibacy asking the Diet to remove obstructions against marriage. Not long afterward, he wrote a sarcastic petition to the bishop of Constance in which he clearly placed the authority of the Scriptures above ecclesiastical thinking.

In January, 1523, there was so much agitation in popular feeling brought on by his papers that it seemed best to the Council of Zurich to arrange a public disputation for the thorough discussion of the subjects. Zwingli developed sixty-seven reformatory arguments[58] which were so convincing that the council charged him to persevere in his evangelical methods, and they made it clear that all other preachers should follow his example.

This was a complete triumph for Zwingli, and it made possible definite steps toward reform. Clergymen married, convents were thrown open, baptismal services were translated, the cathedral chapter (or assembly), which had supported a considerable number of clergy who performed no worthy service was reformed, and the schools under its control were greatly improved.

By October, 1523, a second disputation was held to consider the elimination of the mass and images in the churches. The clergy and people in the country were to be prepared for the change, and meanwhile, excessive zeal was to be held in check. The twelve cantons of the confederacy of Lucerne responded and demanded a return to the old order, but the council of Zurich answered that Zurich would remain true to the confederacy, that the Word of God and the salvation of souls demanded reform, and that a return to the old ways was impossible.

---

[58]The "Sixty-Seven Articles are reproduced by Schaff, Vol. III, p197

Public opinion against the mass and images became so strong, and impatience against delay was so great, that the council gave orders in June, 1524 to destroy the images, giving little time for the instruction of the clergy and people. Another change was made only a few months later, when the Lord's Supper was celebrated without liturgy.

A number of Zwingli's ablest supporters, taught by Zwingli to reject all doctrines not taught in the New Testament, came to the same conclusions as the Anabaptists, that is, to reject infant baptism, to insist on a regenerate membership in the churches, and to deny the right of civil authorities to dictate in matters of religion.

Zwingli seriously considered accepting the same positions, but upon observing the separatism, and the supposed extreme views of the Anabaptists, he was convinced that it would be impractical to follow their example. Thus, he was led to defend infant baptism and to support the system of investing all church authority in the civil council under the advice of the religious leaders of the canton.

Zwingli had the favorable support of a number of influential people in Bern, a good number of whom were also Anabaptist supporters, and some who had begun their work before Luther posted his theses. The authorities in Bern were on the whole favorable toward the reformation, but dreaded agitation. Evangelists who aroused controversy are known to have been banished, while those of milder disposition were allowed to remain.

In Basel, the most important city in Switzerland at that time, was a university that was endowed by the popes and was a great literary center where humanism was gaining considerable ground. Erasmus was there, and was the idol of the learned and noble. The works of Luther were published and circulated all over Europe.

Among a number of evangelicals also there, preaching from the Scriptures, was William Reublin, who later became an Anabaptist. He "interpreted the
Scriptures so well," according to one observer, "that the like had never been heard before."

Reublin preached for about a year, being shielded by his great popularity, but in 1522, with a company of friends, he indulged in a pork-feast on Palm Sunday to show contempt for Church dogmas on feasting. He was held responsible for this outrage, while Erasmus, who regularly ate meat secretly on fast days, condemned him for this show of contempt for the Church. As a result, Reublin was banished, almost causing the people to revolt.

Zwingli's early reformatory preaching aroused great interest among all social and religious reformers of Switzerland, and a large part of the people were ready to cast off the papal yoke and abolish all practices not consistent with the Scriptures.

Zwingli had conferred with Balthasar Hubmaier, a learned and eloquent priest and soon-to-be Anabaptist leader in connection with the disputations that took place to determine how far it was safe to go in the direction of practical reform. Zwingli conceded to Hubmaier, "that children should not be baptized before they are instructed in the faith." Hubmaier was among the earliest, but not the first, in connection with the Swiss Reformation to press the adoption of believer's baptism.

During the latter half of 1523, several others of Anabaptist sympathies had further conferences with Zwingli in which they urged him to take steps toward setting up a pure Church. They pointed out the unseemliness of making church reformation dependent upon the will of an ungodly civil authority and adding them into the fellowship of the Church.

Zwingli was conciliatory and promised to proceed as rapidly as he could, but urged them to be patient, pointing out the disastrous consequences of schism. A large group of radicals kept up persistent agitation, but because of Zwingli's persistence in holding to infant baptism and advocating the rule of civil authority in religious affairs, their trust in Zwingli quickly faded.

By reason of persistent persecution of Anabaptists in Switzerland, their numbers rapidly declined. Some went into Moravia, finding it to be a place of refuge and abounding opportunity.

From 1525 until his death in 1531, Zwingli's time was occupied with controversies with the Lutherans, efforts to suppress the great and popular Anabaptist movement, and military conflict with the Swiss Romanists. His correspondence with evangelical leaders of Switzerland, Southern Germany, and other places shows that he was the trusted leader of the movement and able to control not only the Zurich council and the entire religious government of the canton, but also a large number of other Swiss evangelical communities. At the same time, he was a molding influence on many cities of Southern Germany.

A Swiss Diet controlled by Romanists excommunicated Zwingli. It resolved to bring to an end all changes being made to doctrine and worship and to burn all Protestant versions of the Bible and heretical works of all kinds throughout the confederacy.

With tensions at a high level, five cantons formed a league for mutual defense against Zwinglian aggression and for the re-establishment of Romanism throughout Switzerland. By 1529 the feeling between the two parties was bitter. The burning of Jacob Kaiser, a

Zwinglian who had been evangelizing in Romanists territory, led the Protestants to take the field at once. Zwingli, as the military leader, prepared military instructions, planned the campaign, and took his place side by side with the soldiers.

Conflict was averted by sympathy on both sides for a weeping man, pleading for a delay in fighting, to allow for negotiations that might save the confederacy. The hostile armies established friendly relations, shared provisions, and briefly clung to the notion that the Swiss were one people and not inclined toward shedding the blood of one another.

The parties signed a treaty for mutual toleration, but toleration was to be short-lived when it quickly became clear that both parties misunderstood the provisions of the treaty. . The Catholic cantons raised an army of eight thousand men, and assumed the offensive in October, 1531. The Zurich people and their allies were demoralized with superstitious foreboding. Zwingli, himself, saw the great Halley's Comet and believed it to be a sign of disaster, both for himself and for the evangelical cause.

A pitiful army of only fifteen hundred men could be mustered for battle by a discouraged and despondent Zwingli. In the course of the futile effort, five hundred of the staunchest element in the city and canton, including pastors, members of the councils, and Zwingli, himself, were slain. Zwingli's body was cut into pieces and burned, and his ashes were mingled with those of swine and scattered to the wind.

New leadership arose to work for the consolidation of the churches, but in just a few years the Zwinglian movement would be absorbed by the movement led by John Calvin.

HUBMAIER AND THE ANABAPTISTS

Wilhelm Reublin, an eloquent priest, was driven from Basel in 1522 because of his zeal against papal ceremonies. As pastor at Wytikon, he publicly declared himself opposed to the baptism of infants. Many withheld their children from baptism, and along with Reublin were imprisoned and fined, but the anti-pedobaptist (against the baptism of children) agitation rapidly extended throughout Zurich and the neighboring cantons and provinces.

In Zurich, a large group of religious leaders, led by Conrad Grebel, an accomplished classical and Hebrew scholar, declared themselves against infant baptism. At the close of 1524, they took the decisive step of introducing believers' baptism and organizing churches of the regenerate (born again). Grebel began by baptizing Georg Blaurock, an eloquent social and religious reformer and ex-monk, who in turn baptized a large number. The movement spread rapidly, and within a few weeks multitudes in various parts of Switzerland had received the new baptism.

In May, 1523, Dr. Balthasar Hubmaier, a priest, both learned and eloquent, carrying on a successful reforming movement in the city of Waldshut, in Austria, had expressed his belief to Zwingli that "children should not be baptized before they are instructed in the faith," but he had not yet put believer's baptism into practice. Hubmaier had won overwhelming support in Waldshut by early 1524, but was driven out of the city by Austrian authorities in September and took refuge in Schaffhausen, where, he wrote a tract on "Heretics and their Burners, one of the most thorough-going pleas for liberty of conscience that the age produced.

In early 1525 he discontinued the practice of infant baptism, and by February set forth a "Public Challenge" to all Christian men to prove from Scripture that baptism should be administered to infants. Hubmaier was baptized, along with about sixty others, by Reublin, who visited Waldshut around Easter of that year. Immersion seems not to have been used at that time, for according to a statement made shortly after his own baptism, Hubmaier baptized over three hundred more "out of a milk pail."

A letter by Hubmaier offering an elaborate refutation of the arguments of Œcolampadius and Zwingli (who supported infant baptism0 was published in July. In December, Waldshut fell into the hands of the Austrian authorities after heroic resistance. Hubmaier narrowly escaped and made his way, broken in health, ragged and wretched, to Zurich. There, he was thrown into a prison with more than twenty other starving Anabaptist men and women who were given to understand that there was no escape from this slow starvation except by a denial of their faith. It is thought that Hubmaier was tortured into signing some form of a recantation, for he was at last released to Moravia, where he performed yet a greater work.

Moravia had shared with Bohemia in the Hussite revolt against Rome and in the Bohemian Brethren movements. Their royal government had been weak for about ten years, and many nobles and priests had declared themselves supporters of the reform. Hubmaier was received with open arms at Nickolsburg in the summer of 1526. In a few months he was accepted as leader of the evangelical ministers in that part of Moravia..

In less than a year, from six to twelve thousand had submitted to believers' baptism. Hubmaier was provided with a printing plant, which began to publish his papers, one after another. He was seized by the Austrian authorities in July, 1527, and the following March was burned at the stake.

Anabaptist leaders were for the most part skilled workers in a variety of industries. Their children were carefully brought up and educated in their communal nurseries and schools and were taught trades or agriculture, according to the interest of the community.

The Moravian nobles came to regard them as essential to the prosperity of the country and resisted, as long as they were able, the demands of the Austrian government for their extermination. Severe persecutions occurred in 1535 and from 1547 through 1554.

Beginning in 1592, they suffered almost continuously, and they suffered greatly during the Thirty-Years War. Afterward, they were either destroyed, or they fled before the successive invasions of the Germans, the Turks, and the Tartars. The Jesuits continued throughout as instruments of the persecutions.

THE PEASANTS' WAR

The Peasants' War of 1524-1525 was not the first of its kind. Throughout the later Middle Ages, and in almost every part of Europe, uprisings of greater or less magnitude had taken place. The great mass of the Germanic peoples, noted from ancient times for their love of liberty, had been reduced to a state of serfdom by the feudal system.

Captives of war undoubtedly formed the basis, then poverty and debt brought multitudes of free men into the same condition. The peasants had few rights. In many cases they were bought and sold along with the land. They were required to follow the lord in his warlike enterprises. He could impose any rents or taxes he might see fit, take the peasant's possessions without his consent, or ride over his crops with his hunting parties. Furthermore, the life of the peasant could be taken for any reason, or without a reason, at the whim of his lord.

The clergy scarcely treated the peasants any better-often, worse. Most of the bishops, archbishops, and abbots were members of titled families, and often their motives were purely secular. They usually had to pay a high price for their appointments, and fleecing the peasants was a convenient way to recover the cost.

In August, 1524 Hans Muller, an experienced warrior and orator led 1200 man to Waldshut and formed an evangelical brotherhood with the citizens, who had become strongly democratic in sentiment under the preaching of the great reformer and soon-to-be Anabaptist, Balthasar Hubmaier..

They were resolved to obey no other lord than the emperor, and to destroy all castles, monasteries, and everything ecclesiastical, knowing that castles were a perpetual menace to liberty, and that monasteries could be maintained only at the expense of the tillers of the soil. They were thoroughly convinced that they could expect only taxation and oppression from the clergy.

The Evangelical Brotherhood, thus constituted, sent emissaries far and wide to organize the peasants in every locality. The aim was to bring about a state of society in every respect righteous and in accord with the spirit of the gospel.

The Swabian League, organized for the suppression of insurrection, was soon in a position to cope with the insurgents, but not until the movement had made great headway and almost the whole peasant population of Europe was in arms.

The peasants, during the first quarter of 1525, swept everything before them. They went from town to town in a thoroughly organized manner and carried with them *The Twelve Articles of the Peasants*, which may have been written by Hubmaier. Thomas Carlisle pronounced the *Articles* "worthy of a Solon." An able German historian says, "It was a man of heart and intellect" who composed the articles...."

Many towns were sympathetic and received the peasants with open arms, but the lords were pressed to accept the terms of the Articles or to expect the worst, and in many cases, castles, monasteries, and other religious houses were burned down.

In some instances, especially those under the direct influence of the fanatical Thomas Munzer, the peasants wreaked bloody vengeance upon their lords, and were much inclined to obey Munzer's hysterical exhortation to rush upon the "enemies of the Lord, to slay, slay, and tire not." Munzer claimed that the sword of Gideon was in his hand and that he would lead them on to victory. "On, on, on," he shrieked, "Never mind the wail of the godless...."

The Swabian League fielded a strong force under one of the ablest and cruelest generals of the age. The tide was soon turned, and disaster swept over the entire field. Munzer proved a complete failure. He had provided guns, but neglected the ammunition. He wrought the poor peasants up to a state of frenzy and led them to the false hope of a miraculous intervention.

Over all, about one hundred thousand miserable people were butchered by the troops of the League. The failure of the Peasants Revolt can be attributed to the actions of Munzer. His actions, which were carried on with carnal expectations of setting up the Kingdom of

God on earth by means of force, were a deadly poison, as it would be to any movement.

The fact that the *Twelve Articles*, themselves, being far in advance of the religious thinking of the time, may have been an additional reason for failure, but the truths expressed in the *articles* are immortal and have been abundantly justified through history. Today, the demands of the peasants would be considered reasonable and just, and would be readily accepted.

Thomas Munzer is usually regarded as the forerunner of the Anabaptist movement, although he was never really an Anabaptist. He rejected infant baptism in theory, but held on to it in practice. He seems never to have submitted to believers' baptism, nor to have re-baptized others, but his influence upon some Anabaptist parties was great, and other campaigns patterned after his behavior were attempted. His actions were prejudicial toward the more soundly Biblical Anabaptists, who were blamed and greatly abused because of Munzer.

JOHN CALVIN IN GENEVA

John Calvin was given a benefice for his education at the age of twelve. Two years later, he was sent to Paris to study classics and philosophy. His admirable success in his studies made possible his appointment, at the age of eighteen, to an important position entrusted with the salvation of souls, but he had not thought of the salvation of his own soul.

He came under the influence of the German Reformation, but because of his reverence for the Church, he long resisted reformatory teachings. In 1533, at the age of twenty-four, he revealed that he had experienced a sudden conversion. Within the next two years, his *Insti-*

tutes of the Christian Religion,[59] a masterpiece, was issued from the press, and it placed the youth of twenty-seven "in the foremost ranks of the theological thinkers of the ages."

Geneva had hardly been affected by the Zwinglian reforms that took place in Zurich and Berne, but it was soon to become the Protestant stronghold, not only for Switzerland, but for the world. Some evangelists had been working in Geneva in 1536, when a patriotic party overthrew the authority of a bishop of the established Church. The evangelists sensed that the time had come for an intense evangelistic effort in Geneva, and they were convinced that strong leadership was needed.

It seemed providential that just after Calvin's famous *Institutes* was published, he came through Geneva on his was to Strasbourg. William Farel convinced him of the urgent need for leadership to save the city for evangelical Christianity and pressed upon him his conviction that "God's curse would rest upon him if he should turn his back on this great opportunity for service." The appeal felt too strong for Calvin to resist, and he accepted Farel's invitation as the voice of God.

Although Calvin built upon Zwinglian foundations, he had little respect for Zwingli, who had been content to carry on his reformation under the auspices of civil authorities. Calvin rejected such a role for the Church and insisted that the Church must not only be independent of the State, but that it must rule the State.

Calvin was more organized in his thinking and had far better administrative ability than any other Protestant leader and firmly believed that his cause was the cause of God, and he absolutely refused to compromise his

---

[59]Further described by Schaff, Vol. I, pp.444-466

almost total authority to carry out what he supposed was his divinely appointed mission.

Within a few months, he had demonstrated his masterful ability and was recognized as the spiritual leader of the canton. A new system of Church order was presented to the council that provided for strict enforcement of Church discipline. It included provisions for spying on all citizens, the reporting of moral and religious delinquencies, and providing punishment by civil penalties and excommunication. Thus, Calvin led in the establishment of a theocracy more demanding of moral and religious behavior than even the Jewish and the Roman theocracies of ancient times.

The Genevan people had been struggling for years for civil and religious liberty at great sacrifice, and now to be brought under the galling yoke of a theocracy with foreign preachers as the dictators seemed to be more than they could bear. Attempts were made to convince Calvin and Farel to ease the severity of the disciplinary measures of the system, but they refused to compromise. As a result, Calvin's opponents gained the power to have them banished from Geneva in 1538.

The new regime utterly failed to prevent anarchy and bring peace to the city. Because of their failure, Calvin's friends felt that he, alone, could give the city the religious and political government that was needed. They soon regained control and sent out an invitation for his return.

Calvin felt that if he returned, he must carry out his theocratic idea in the face of all opposition. To allow heretics to preach their error, to him, would be as inexcusable as to allow the spread of contagious disease when it could be prevented. For his examples, he looked to the God-approved and faithful kings of the

Old Testament who remorselessly suppressed idolatry and destroyed all their worshippers.

Calvin came back to Geneva 1541 and was given an ovation as he entered the city. From that time onward, he was in a position to dictate the terms of his leadership and would be content with no half-way measures. A theocracy, pure and simple, with remorseless punishment, even unto death, was his program for the opponents of the theocracy and teachers of false doctrines.

The rigor with which Calvin's ordinances were carried out soon brought forth a storm of protest, but no mercy was shown to the opposition. New methods of torture were introduced, and the obstinate were given to understand that, unless they yielded, their days would be ended in torment. A system of espionage was introduced to prevent secret transgression. Informers shared fines, and the testimony of children against parents was readily accepted. During the years 1542 to 1546, fifty-eight executions occurred and seventy-six people were banished. During the pestilence of 1545, alone, thirty-four women were burned or quartered on suspicion of spreading the plague by means of magic.

Calvin's humiliation of political opponents, and the execution of one, still further intensified the opposition against him, but by the sheer force of his personality, he triumphed, and his position was greatly strengthened by the arrival in Geneva of large companies of zealous and devoted followers from France and other parts of Europe who sought refuge from persecution.

A final uprising against Calvin and his foreign supporters resulted in complete defeat of the opposition and the execution of some of its leaders. From that time until his death in 1563, his authority was almost undisputed.

The aggressive teachings of Calvin gradually became dominant in the Zwinglian cantons. It spread into some provinces of Germany and the Netherlands, and a constant stream of zealous missionaries flowed from Geneva into France.

THE HUGUENOTS IN FRANCE

The Calvinist movement in France (the Huguenots) grew rapidly, and in spite of the loss of thousands by persecution, about fifty churches could be assembled by 1559 for the organization of their forces. They adopted a Calvinistic confession of faith and a system of Church order based on that of Calvin, but the confession of the Huguenots was more democratic in character.

A system of synods was inaugurated to settle differences between parties, beginning with a consistory, or governing board, in each church. Differences involving more than one church were to be settled in provincial synods, and a national synod was called for, which would be the highest court of appeal.

After the Huguenots had struggled for religious liberty under the extreme Romanist party for forty years and had endured attempts for their extermination by massacre and three bloody religious wars, a king rose to power who was sympathetic to their cause.

Henry of Navarre, the son of a Protestant, was the most legitimate successor, yet he had to fight his way to the throne against the combined powers of the Catholics of both Spain and France. He received some aid from the struggling Netherlands, from England, and from Germany, but only by coming to terms with the pope and declaring himself to be a Catholic was he able to gain the support that he needed.

Ascending to the throne in 1594, Henry of Navarre secured for the Protestants most of the rights for which they had so long struggled and suffered, but because he had returned to the Roman Church, himself, he made it almost certain that Romanism would regain the power to stamp out the new faith.

Through the Edict of Nantes, of 1598, Henry granted complete liberty of conscience, but Protestant worship was limited to places where it was already practiced, with few exceptions. Because of such restrictions, active evangelism was out of the question.

Continuation of the limited provisions of the Edict depended almost entirely on the will of the monarch. One by one, the Protestant privileges were taken away, leaving their conditions more and more intolerable.

The Romanists had all the tools of aggression in their own hands. The Jesuits were at work there, as everywhere, with their diabolical practices, and the Protestants could hope for no better than a gradual extinction.

In October 1685, Louis XIV, who early in his reign had been sympathetic toward the Protestants, issued a "perpetual and irrevocable edict," depriving the Protestants of all privileges and made it necessary to renounce the faith, suffer martyrdom, or flee the realm.

Large numbers emigrated to England, Holland, Germany, Switzerland, and America. Hundreds of thousands renounced their faith and many thousands suffered martyrdom. A smaller number secretly remained and were able, after the tempest of the persecution had somewhat abated, to reorganize their forces.

The French Reformed Church may be seen as represented by an old seal that has been preserved with an image of the burning bush of Moses and this motto: *"Flagror, sed non conburor"* (burned, but not consumed) and a notation indicating that these words support the tragic history of the Church.[60]

THE SCOTTISH REFORMATION

Scotland was evangelized by British missionaries in ancient times, and the early form of Christianity survived without significant change until Hildebrand imposed the Roman form of Christianity upon the land in the eleventh century. Scotland gained independence from England in 1314 with the encouragement of the pope and the aid of the French king, and Roman sway became complete.

The works of Wycliffe and Huss were the beginning of reformatory influences upon Scotland. After the burning of a Lollard preacher in 1407 and a Hussite Bohemian in 1432, there was strong sentiment in favor of reform among all classes.

Several notable predecessors of John Knox were well-educated. They had been influenced by Erasmus and the reformatory work of Luther. Among them was Patrick Hamilton, whose preaching and teaching were ardent and earnest, but he was soon condemned for heresy and died heroically at the stake in February of 1528.

By the early 1540's, the Protestants were growing at a rapid rate, and it was about then that George Wishart, also an influential predecessor of Knox, was banished for teaching the Greek language and having Protestant inclinations. In 1544, after spending some years at the University of Cambridge, he returned to Scotland to preach the gospel. Knox, who was soon to become the leader of the Scottish Reformation, became

---

[60]Schaff, Vol. II, p.492.

devotedly attached to Wishart and sometimes accompanied him, sword in hand, to protect him from violence on his preaching tours. Described as a man of loveliness and apostolic zeal, Wishart was tried, condemned, and burned in March 1546. His martyrdom gave fresh impetus to the Protestant cause.

John Knox was born in 1505 and educated at the university of St. Andrews, where he studied and taught scholastic philosophy. He was converted to Protestantism about 1542 and quietly promoted the cause of Protestantism, but after the death of Wishart he preached and taught boldly and effectively. He was captured by the French in 1547 and held in France as a galley slave for nineteen months. Due to the influence of the English, he was released in 1549 and worked in England for the Protestant cause until 1554, when he was driven away by the persecuting zeal of Queen Mary.

Knox then went to Geneva to become personally acquainted with John Calvin. For one year he was pastor of a congregation of English exiles in Frankfort-on-the-Main, where he was accused of treason for writing against the emperor. He, then, returned to Geneva and worked zealously writing tracts and letters, assisting in the preparation of the new Genevan version of the Bible, and writing other documents in preparation for his return to Scotland.

War with England, Knox's letters and published writings, and the martyrdom of an aged priest in 1558 gave encouragement to the Protestants. The Scottish nobles, who had little interest in maintaining the papacy, had much interest in its abolition. Their interests included a desire to take over Church property. A large number of nobles who had become Protestants made a solemn covenant, wherein they pledged to maintain, protect, and defend the "whole congregation of Christ, and every member thereof...."

It was by this covenant that Knox was encouraged to return to Scotland. As he began preaching with irresistible zeal, the people were wrought up to a feverish pitch and began the destruction of shrines and images in the houses of worship. A civil war began, which resulted in triumph for the Protestants in 1560. Parliament promptly ratified a Confession of Faith and a summary of doctrines, strictly Calvinistic in nature, written by John Knox.[61] These articles served as a confessional standard until the Westminster Assembly set forth the same doctrines more elaborately in 1647.[62]

THE ENGLISH REFORMATION

HENRY VIII (1509-1547)

By the beginning of the reign of Henry VIII in 1509, Parliament, which had been powerful in the past, was now rarely called together. It was part of Henry's policy to crush out what remained of the liberty of the people in order to make his own sovereignty complete. An understanding existed between Henry VIII and the pope. Henry would uphold the pope in all wars with the emperor, the king of France, and with Luther and would enjoy the right of making all ecclesiastical nominations in England.. In return, the pope would favor Henry's claims on French territory, confirm his ecclesiastical appointments, and bestow upon him the title *Defender of the Faith*.

Few rulers ever reigned in Europe who were more absolute despots than Henry VIII, and few rulers have

---

[61] Schaff, Vol. III, p. 437
[62] Schaff, Vol. III, p. 600

ever had less regard for the rights of others. No crime was too flagrant, if it seemed to be in his interest or for his pleasure. He was somewhat superstitious in his regard for the Roman religion, but to him, like many of his day, religion was absolutely divorced from personal morality, and it did not keep him from breaking with the papacy when it suited his purpose.

The king was reluctant to aggravate either the pope or the Romanizing party in England, for fear of an uprising by the masses, whom the priests and monks might incite to rebellion. To insure moderation in the king's treatment of the Protestants, Thomas Cranmer, an advisor to Henry, and a friend of the Reformation, strove to impress upon him the fact that papal doctrines and practices rest on the same foundation as papal supremacy, and that the only way to limit papal power and gain immunity from its exercise, was to encourage Protestantism.

Henry's despair, due to the death of his sons and the absence of a legitimate male successor, encouraged a sense of divine disapproval of his marriage. His growing antipathy toward Catherine, who had lost her charms through age and ill health and his passion for the young and fascinating Anne Boleyn, led him to seek a divorce. He must find a way of annulling his marriage, but this would not be an easy task, for Catherine had been his wife for fifteen years. Further, it was not to his advantage that the emperor was her nephew.

Emperor Charles V sacked Rome and took the pope prisoner, leaving him in dire need of Henry's friendship, but he dared not comply with his request for an annulment for fear of antagonizing the emperor and making his own condition worse. After four years of seeking an annulment from the pope, Henry was exasperated beyond measure. Cranmer assured him that by seeking the opinion of learned men of the universities throughout Europe, he would find a reason for the annulment of his marriage.

Cranmer wrote a book to prove that Levitical law forbade marriage to a deceased brother's widow. Since that is what Henry had done when he married Catherine, it was thought that Henry's marriage should be considered against Scripture, and should be annulled to clear the way for his marriage to Anne. Clerics and theologians throughout Europe were found who agreed with Cranmer, and their support was successful in winning Henry's confidence.

Thomas Cromwell, a political advisor to Henry, seems to have aimed only at complete despotic power for the king. He advised Henry that the Church is only a department of the State and that Henry ought to take the matter into his own hands and declare himself head of the Church within his realm.

By the end of the year 1532, and after further and fruitless efforts to secure the annulling of his marriage from Rome, Henry was privately married, according to his wishes. Soon afterward, Cranmer became Archbishop of Canterbury. He quickly declared Henry's marriage to Catherine null from the beginning and the marriage to Anne Boleyn to be lawful.

In 1534, Parliament passed *The Act of Supremacy.* It made the king and his heirs and successors supreme head, on earth, of the Church of England. Cromwell, though not a priest, was made vicar-general of the Church, and the bishops and clergy were made utterly subservient to his rule. Not only were ecclesiastical duties specified exactly, but the time and subject-matter of their sermons and discourses as well. Spies were generally on hand to report the slightest hint of dissatisfaction against the government.

The *Court of the Star Chamber,* representing the absolute civil and ecclesiastical power of the king, became, in Cromwell's hands, a terror to England. The king, in order to prove he was no heretic, persecuted the Protestants as vigorously as he persecuted the Catholics who refused to recognize him as head of the Church in England. Hundreds of the greatest and noblest men and women of England were victims of the policy, including Queen Anne Boleyn, who had done what she could to encourage the Protestants. She was beheaded in 1536.

During the late 1530's, Henry closed the monasteries, giving encouragement to the Protestants, but it caused a rebellion of the monks, after which, the leaders were put to death. He went so far as to destroy the images and shrines in the churches. He confiscated the abbey lands and began to allow unrestrained reading of the English Bible, but the influential Romanizing party in the royal court took every opportunity to prejudice him against Protestantism.

Henry soon became displeased with Cranmer and the other high-ranking Protestants for making the objection that the king was taking all the abbey lands for royal use. They insisted that large portions be used for theological seminaries, grammar schools, hospitals and workhouses wherever needed.

By 1539, the king, growing more hostile to Protestantism, upheld most of the doctrines of the Roman Church and called for the enactment of six *Bloody Articles.* These *Articles* declared as heresy any denial of transubstantiation and some other Roman doctrines and made it punishable by death,. Persistent efforts were made by the Romanizers to suppress the English Bible, but its reading continued, and the Protestant Party steadily gained ground until the death of the king in 1547.

EDWARD VI (1547-1553)

Henry had cut off the pope's authority in England, but he was not always kind to the Protestants, and Protestantism did not become the state religion until Edward VI came to power. Edward was Henry's son by his third wife, Jane Seymour, whom he married in 1536, the same year Anne Boleyn was beheaded. He was brought up as a Protestant, with Thomas Cranmer as head of the regency, and became king in 1547 at the age of nine.

Cramner had virtually become a Calvinist. As he began to carry out his plans for governing, he removed the Romanizing bishops from office and replaced them with Protestants. He brought many theologians to England from the continent to teach in the universities and to aid in organizing the Protestant movement. John Knox assisted after he was liberated from forced labor on a French galley, and Calvin corresponded frequently with Cranmer and the king.

Laws were made effective to repeal the *Bloody Articles,* to remove images from the churches, to allow the clergy to marry, and to substitute tables for altars. Laws against Lollard teachings were eliminated, and translations of the writings of the leading reformers of Europe were freely circulated.

Cranmer and Ridley, an associate introduced an English version of *the Book of Common Prayer* and Protestant articles of faith. Many Romish elements without Scriptural warrant were retained in *The Book of Common Prayer* to conciliate the great mass of the clergy and people who were still addicted to popish superstitions and inclined to resist the simplicity of Calvinistic worship. Although it was little more than a translation of parts of the Roman breviary, its solemn music and powerful style made a strong appeal to wavering hearts.[63]

Cranmer's policy was one of great moderation, and he argued that while traditions are to be rejected in matters of faith, custom is often a good argument for the continuance of what has been long used in matters of rites and ceremonies.

MARY TUDOR (BLOODY MARY)

Mary, Queen of England from 1553 to 1558, the daughter of Henry VIII and Catherine of Aragon, had steadfastly remained a Roman Catholic. The harsh treatment she had received from Henry and Edward deeply embittered her against Protestantism. Her advisors, who were representatives of the pope, had impressed upon her mind that it was her duty, if she ever became sovereign, to blot out heresy from her realm.

Once established in power, she promptly repealed all the anti-papal legislation of Henry and Edward, restored much of the confiscated church property, and condemned to death a large number of the Protestant leaders, including Cranmer. Thousands of other Protestants and English evangelicals took refuge in the Netherlands, Germany, Geneva, and other places on the continent.

The actual number of victims of Mary's reign may have been small number in comparison with the victims of the Counter-Reformation in such countries as the Netherlands, Austria, and France, but it has been well said that "the excesses of this bloody reaction accomplished more for making England Protestant than all the efforts put forth under Edward's reign."

---

[63]Boak, Hyma, and Slosson,, The Growth of the European Civilization,

A large number of the brightest intellects of England spent the years of their exile in mastering the principles of Calvinism. Upon the death of Mary, they were as one mind, determined to return to England to establish a Christian theocracy.

ELIZABETH (1558-1603)

Elizabeth, the daughter of Henry VIII and Anne Boleyn was brought up as a Protestant, but partly as a measure of prudence, under the reign of Mary, she outwardly conformed to the Catholic religion until her position as queen was fully assured. Even after ascending to the throne in 1558, she was cautious, for fear of antagonizing the Catholic Church, which could provoke Spain and France into supporting Mary Stuart, Queen of the Scots, in her pretensions to the English crown.

Elizabeth revealed her preferences in the opening of her first Parliament, which included the celebration of the Mass and the preaching of an evangelical sermon. At first she moved slowly, but it didn't take her long to realize that her interests lay in the adoption of Protestantism, and that it was the course she had to take. She quickly added eight evangelicals to her council and Bonner, the chief agent of Mary's bloody measures was ignored. Her favorable attitude toward the new faith was a sign that prompted thousands of exiles to return to England.

She accepted as her policy a proposal by one of her counselors that the Church of England be "reduced to its former purity" (the way it was before of Queen Mary), but her policy was shaped by her preference for the Catholic order of worship and her inclination to pay little attention to the Puritan reformers. From the beginning, she determined that those who had been prominent in Mary's service be gradually "abased," and those who had been enriched by Mary's favor be compelled to restore their wealth to the crown.

The most characteristic feature of English Protestantism was the half-hearted nature and compromising disposition of its leadership. The rulers of the Century, like Elizabeth, insisted on rule by arbitrary power and would tolerate no contradiction. As a result, it was men of feeble conviction and flexible conscience that shaped the policy of the English Church and fixed its character.

The committee to revise the *Prayer Book* was strongly evangelical in its sentiment, but Elizabeth was anxious to satisfy moderate Catholics, and most of the ceremonial provisions were retained, but some, such as kneeling to receive the elements and prayers for the dead were rejected by the committee,. Significant among the omissions, was the prayer,

> "From all sedition and privy conspiracy, from the tyranny of the bishop of Rome and all his detestable enormities ... good Lord, deliver us."

On the other hand, the theologians had been educated under the influence of German Protestantism, and something decidedly Protestant was demanded for them. That something could be provided in the form of a creed. The *Articles* were, therefore, drawn up in the Protestant spirit and were based on examples of Protestant formulas existing at the time.[64]

The establishment of two separate spiritual guides was an attempt to make the Anglican Church acceptable to both Protestants and those favoring the Roman liturgy, but it laid the foundation of antagonism between the

---

[64]These Articles are reproduced by Schaff, Vol.III,p.486.

two parties. There was a constant struggle between those who interpreted the *Articles* by the *Prayer Book* and those who interpreted the *Prayer Book* by the *Articles*

In January, 1559, Parliament restored to the crown supreme authority in ecclesiastical matters with the right to nominate a Court of High Commission for ensuring compliance with the queen's supreme authority. In the same year, *the Act of Uniformity* was adopted, making exclusive use of the revised liturgy (*Prayer Book*) a universal obligation.

Mary Stuart, supported by France, and to some extent Spain, along with part of the English nobility, attempted to deprive Elizabeth of her throne in 1569. Conspiracies against Elizabeth's life and a pronouncement against her as an apostate, supposedly fostered by the pope, brought her into open warfare with the papacy, but the Queen of the Scots was forced to flee her own country before the wrath of a great number who accused her of murdering her first husband, Henry Stuart, shortly after which, she married the Earl of Bothwell.[65] She sought the protection of Elizabeth, who imprisoned her, then, in 1587, ordered her execution for treason.

From 1569 onward, colleges for the education of missionaries to England were established in three cities of Europe, including one in Rome, and by 1585 as many as three hundred priests are said to have come secretly to England to propagate their faith and to overthrow England's great queen.

In 1588, there was an attempt by the Spanish Armada to invade England, but its destruction by the British fleet brought an end to Spanish interference in the affairs of Elizabeth and completed the triumph of Protestantism

---

[65]Boak, Vol. II, p. 47.

in England. Elizabeth's long reign resulted in the almost complete displacement of Roman Catholicism, which at the beginning was the dominant form of religion, but her Protestant subjects had become hopelessly divided.

Bishop Bancroft, who was soon to become archbishop and political advisor to James I, first expressed the views in 1589 that would lay the foundation of the High Church party that was soon to come forth with great strength and aggressiveness. He upheld the divine right and exclusive validity of episcopacy, saying that no other form of church government had ever been dreamed of from the days of the apostles until the time of the Puritans. The constituents of the High Church party were those who favored a return to Romanism, but could be appeased by the use of some elements of the Roman form of worship.

A large and intelligent group who were radically opposed to separation from the established Church felt it wise to conform for the time, hoping for an eventual reformation on a Calvinistic basis. These Puritans would long afterward be known as the Low Church, or evangelical party. The belief of Bancroft that the very nature of Presbyterianism led them to rebel against rulers was the basis of their persecution.

The third division of Protestants included the Separatists and Puritans who refused to conform. From 1534 onward, there had been small bodies of Anabaptists, usually from the continent, and Mennonite types who were often arraigned before the authorities to be banished or burned. They were the beginnings of the great dissenting bodies that have been such a strong part of the religious life of England and her colonies, especially in North America.

One Separatist church formed in the time of Elizabeth was one established by Robert Browne, about 1578.

Browne had reached the conviction that Presbyterianism had no more scriptural support than Episcopacy. He believed that the example of the apostles required the formation of local churches absolutely independent of one another, and that each local body should be a pure democracy, and that the Lord Jesus Christ should be its only head.

It is highly probable that Browne was in some measure indebted for his advanced views on congregationalism, the separation of church and state, and his reliance on scriptural authority to the Mennonites, who abounded in this region at the time.

Queen Elizabeth, because of her strength, was able to have her way and was able to enforce a rigorous uniformity in opposition to the wishes of a large majority of the people and against the judgment of some of her ablest statesmen.

JAMES I (1603-1625)

James was the son of Mary Stuart, Queen of the Scots, and Henry Stuart. He succeeded his mother in 1587 and became King of Scotland as James VI. Being a descendent of Henry VII of England, he was also next in line to the English throne. In 1603, upon the death of Elizabeth, he became King of England as James I, without opposition.

King James had a good theological education. He had endured, without great difficulty, the domineering of the Scotch Presbyterian Establishment and was confidently expected by the Puritans of England to strongly support their cause.

The king granted the Puritans request for certain additions to the catechism, and he authorized a revision of the English Bible, which was issued in 1611 as the

Authorized, or King James Version. The Puritans soon changed their minds about benefiting from support of the king when their petition to replace the popish elements of church worship with hyper-Calvinistic articles of faith was met with an angry response. His outburst expressed the attitude, not only of himself, but also of Elizabeth, his predecessor, and of Charles I, his successor, and it foreshadowed the departure of thousands of Puritans from England and the eventual flight of the Pilgrim Fathers to Holland and America."[66]

James was thoroughly convinced the theocratic view of the Presbyterians was inconsistent with royal absolutism and that the divine right of kings could best be safeguarded by the recognition of the divine right of bishops as well. With Bancroft as archbishop and chief political advisor to James from 1605 to 1611, nonconforming Puritans and Separatists were subject to severe abuses, such as fines and imprisonment that deprived them of their rights established by law.

Judges who released citizens from jail, trying to protect them from the abuses of the High Commission Court, were arrested and severely fined. Bancroft had persuaded the king that he had a right to coerce judges against taking these actions..

In 1610, Parliament censured the High Court Commission for their abuses and demanded restoration of the Puritan ministers. It was evident that Parliament was more than sympathetic with the Puritan cause and that the old spirit of British liberty had become thoroughly reawakened.

Puritans enjoyed considerable ease under the more moderate administration of Archbishop Abbot beginning in 1611 Being a thoroughgoing Calvinist, Abbot had

---

[66]Boak, II, 100.

little inclination to enforce the Act of Uniformity and many Puritans who had been in exile returned to England under his encouragement, but such encouragement, apparently, did not apply to the Separatists. Consistent with his Calvinistic principles, he seems to have favored the burning of heretics.

About 1618, James' attitude took a sharp turn in favor of the Catholic position. His desire for the marriage of his son, Charles, to the daughter of the King of Spain caused him to refuse support to his son-in-law, Frederick, who was at war against Ferdinand for the Bohemian crown. He, also, began to treat Roman Catholicism in England with a great deal of consideration, but would do nothing for the Puritans.

THE SEPARATISTS UNDER JAMES

In the early years of James' reign, about 1606, John Smyth, a Cambridge graduate, felt compelled to separate from the established Church and consequently gathered a little congregation of Separatists at Gainsborough. Near the same time, John Robinson became pastor of a closely associated congregation at Scrooby Manor, nearby. To these two congregations belonged a number of men who were to become famous in both the New World and the old. Both flocks soon followed large numbers of other Nonconformists and Separatists to the Netherlands, where they had taken refuge and had formed congregations.

By 1608, Smyth and his associates found themselves in disagreement with the pastors of an older Congregational church at Amsterdam. They had reached the conviction that their baptisms were invalid due to being administered in a church practicing infant baptism, which they considered to be an apostate church.

Accordingly, they repudiated their own church organization and their own baptisms, as being inconsistent with regenerate church membership and introduced believer's baptism anew. Smyth, it is said, first baptized himself, and then others. They then reorganized the church, with Smyth as its pastor. (Immersion seems not to have been practiced at this time.)

Smyth and a majority of the flock soon became convinced that they had made a mistake in introducing baptism anew when a body of baptized believers, the Mennonites, could have given them a legitimate baptism.

He and his followers then sought admission into the Mennonite church, but Helwys, Murton, and a few others, breaking fellowship with the majority, insisted on the legitimacy of the proceedings and regarded with great disfavor Smyth's craving for apostolic succession in baptism. The Mennonite church, being exceedingly cautious and fearful of disturbing their own fellowship, postponed final admission of the church into fellowship until 1614, three years after Smyth's death.

Robinson and his flock settled at Leyden. By 1618 conditions of life at Leyden were found to be so severe as to make their very survival extremely doubtful. It was finally arranged, through friends in England, that they should take passage to New England. It required the greatest sacrifices on the part of all to arrange for the transportation for only a part of the congregation. It was arranged that the pastor would go
or stay with the majority, and as the majority remained behind, he finished his life at Leyden.

The party bound for New England landed at Plymouth, Massachusetts in 1620, after suffering untold hardships. Nearly half of those who completed the voyage succumbed during the first winter from lack of proper food and poor protection from the severe weather.

In 1616, A highly educated Puritan minister, Henry Jacob, who had been pastor of an exiled congregation at Middelburg, in Zeeland (of The Netherlands), felt it his duty to spend his life in an effort to establish a pure church in the neighborhood of London. His congregation suffered much persecution, but the church endured to became the mother of most of the Congregational and Baptist churches in England.

CHARLES I (1625-1649)

During the early years of Charles' reign, thousands of Puritans emigrated to New England. In 1628, a colony of non-conforming Puritans settled at Salem, Massachusetts. This colony was greatly reinforced in 1629, in the same year that a far larger and more important colony was planted on Massachusetts Bay. In a few years the Massachusetts Bay Colony had several thousand members, including some leaders who would play an important role in early American history.

The Massachusetts Bay colonists claimed to be loyal churchmen and considered it an honor to call the Church of England their dear mother. Even the Salem men declined to be regarded as Separatists, but soon the force of circumstances led both colonies to reconsider and come to strong Separatist positions.

The Massachusetts Bay colony proceeded to establish a theocracy like that of Geneva, and from 1633 onward, to establish colonies in Connecticut, strongly Presbyterian in sentiment. A colony in New Haven was established by a company of London Puritans under the leadership of John Davenport, in 1637.

Providence was founded in 1636 by Roger Williams, a zealous Separatist, who had so irritated the Massachusetts authorities that he was banished. He denounced the requirement of a citizen's oath of allegiance and opposed the theocratic government and its inherent intolerance and disregard for the consciences of its subjects. It was formed on the basis of absolute liberty of conscience. Williams had become convinced that infant baptism is without scriptural warrant, and with a company of others, he introduced baptism anew and organized the first Baptist church in America in 1639.

In 1638, a group of men and women who were forced to leave Massachusetts because of their disagreements with the standing order settled in Rhode Island. Led by William Coddington and John Clarke, they drew up a constitution which was theocratic in nature, but in 1641, under the influence of Roger Williams, they declared their government to be a democracy and proclaimed the principle of liberty of conscience.

Williams and Clarke secured a charter for the union of Providence and the Rhode Island towns as Providence Plantation, with democracy and liberty of conscience embodied in explicit terms.

King Charles perpetuated the civil and ecclesiastical policy of his father. Devoid of the thorough grounding in Calvinism that James had enjoyed, and with far less education, he was more deeply assured than his father had been of the absoluteness of his authority and his divine right to rule. He was persuaded by his advisers that the correct policy lay in an unwavering assertion of irresponsible authority and the disregard of Parliament and the constitutional rights of the people.

With thorough-going High Churchman, William Laud, as advisor, Parliament was dissolved, and seventeen canons were made effective that asserted divine right of the king to unlimited power and entitlement to the possessions of his subjects without their consent.

Further, there was imposed upon the clergy a requirement to swear, never by counsel or act, "to alter the government of this church by archbishops, deans, and archdeacons, etc." It was called the "*Etcetera Oath*," and bound the clergy to they knew not what. The furor that this policy aroused caused it to be suspended, but after long years of abuse, it was inevitable that the Scottish (Presbyterian) Covenanters would now join hands with the English Puritans against their common enemies.

The Puritan dominated Parliament made a "Solemn League and Covenant" in 1643, in which they agreed, in return for military assistance, to introduce uniformity of religion in England, Scotland, and Ire-land, "according to the example of the best Reformed (Presbyterian) churches." The Parliamentarians defeated the king's army at Marston Moor, July 2, 1644 and a church assembly was convoked at Westminster, which drew up the *Westminster Confession*, and Parliament ordered the abolition of episcopacy throughout England[67].

Now that Presbyterianism had triumphed, the men in control of Parliament foolishly supposed that their own sort of intolerance would prove acceptable, where other varieties had been resisted. The majority of soldiers would tolerate neither episcopacy nor popery. Oliver Cromwell, their leader, organized a cavalry regiment to end what they regarded as the intolerance of Presbyterianism. "Brethren," said Cromwell to his soldiers, "in things of the mind, we look for no compulsion but that of light and reason."

Finally, in 1648, one of the commanders in the army of Independents appeared in the House of Commons

---

[67]Boak, II, 107,108.

and arrested 143 Presbyterian members. The remaining members, about 60, then appointed a *High Court of Justice*, which sentenced Charles to death on the charge of treason, and the king was beheaded on January 30, 1649.

THE COMMONWEALTH AND THE RESTORATION

At first, Cromwell's genius and resolution crushed all opposition in England, Ireland, and Scotland. On the ruins of the monarchy and Parliament, he raised a military government which inspired respect and fear at home and abroad, but which created no affection and love, except among his invincible army.

The man of blood and iron was the ablest ruler that England ever had, but he died at the height of his power. The Puritan Commonwealth was but a brilliant military episode and died with its founder after only 10 years. His amiable and good-natured son, Richard succeeded him and tried to carry on, but he was weak and incompetent, and resigned after only a few months.

The execution of Charles was, in the eyes of the great majority of the English and Scotch people, a crime and a blunder. It became the driving force that would unite the national sentiment in the three kingdoms in demanding restoration of the old dynasty, which was followed shortly by a full restoration of the Episcopacy, which was embraced to an extent as never before.[68]

REFORMATION IN THE NETHERLANDS

By the time of the Reformation, the Netherlands had been affected by the influence of almost every form of medieval evangelical Christianity, including the Waldenses and the Brethren of the Common Life. Hu-

---

[68]Schaff, I, 719-721.

manism, under the influence of Erasmus, gained a firm foothold, then both Lutheranism and Zwinglianism gained a considerable following, but were so bitterly antagonistic that they largely neutralized one another.

By 1529, the popular Anabaptist movement became dominant, and by 1553 a group of Anabaptists under the leadership of Menno came to be known as Mennonites and were by far the most numerous and influential of the evangelical parties. From that time, because of the persecutions under Queen Mary, large numbers of English Protestants took refuge in the Netherlands and greatly furthered the Calvinist cause.

The Netherlands were a part of the possessions inherited by the Spanish emperor, Charles V (1519-1556), who carefully guarded against the encroachments of Protestantism, but a considerable measure of toleration prevailed during the latter part of his reign due to his choice of leaving the provinces under the regency of his sister while he pursued his preference for living in Spain.

Charles' son, Philip II, who succeeded him as king of Spain in 1556, had been trained by the Jesuits to pursue, above all other interests, the extermination of Protestantism. Just as the growth of dissent in the twelfth and thirteenth centuries brought forth the Franciscan and Dominican Orders to search out and destroy heretics, so the Protestant Revolution called forth the Jesuits, who would represent the most enthusiastic Jesuits, who would represent the most enthusiastic, aggressive, and intolerant segment of the Church, thoroughly organized for action. It should be no surprise that the country of Ferdinand and Isabella, who established the inquisition to drive out the Mohammedans and Jews and brought forth Xemines to complete the extirpation of heretical modes of thought, would give to the Church its leaders, organization, and methods for opposing the Protestant Revolution. It was considered necessary that all resources be applied, and the utmost effort be made, to preserve the presumed right of the Church to be regarded as catholic (or universal).

When Philip II came into power, he set up fourteen new dioceses for tighter control of the provinces and posted his placards against heretics throughout the country. He required total exclusion of heresy and unconditional acceptance of the Catholic faith.

A Spanish army began its work of destroying all opposition to Spanish and Catholic authority and by 1573 had spread desolation everywhere. By way of an atrocity rarely equaled, eighteen thousand Evangelicals were massacred. The southern provinces (or Belgium) were, in just a few years, almost cleared of their Protestant populations and chose to remain loyal to Spain.

The Evangelical cause in the northern provinces rapidly gained strength and formed the Union of Utrecht, with William of Orange as the first military leader. Under his leadership, and that of his two sons, assisted by of the English and the French, they eventually won their independence. The Netherlands greatly prospered, and several great universities were founded which became strongholds of Calvinism.

THE COUNTER-REFORMATION

NEGLECTED BY THE POPES

For a generation after Luther published his theses, little was done by the established Church to counteract the Revolution. The popes were too engrossed in their personal pleasure and family interests to care about either the internal reform of the Church or the punishment of those considered guilty of upbraiding the Church.

Leo X, who was pope from 1513 to 1521, was the son of Lorenzo de Medici, the Magnificent, the famous patron of literature and art. He was brought up in a humanistic atmosphere, and his education was purely secular. At the age of eight he was made archbishop of Aix by the king of France on purely political grounds. At thirteen he became a cardinal, and by sixteen he became an active member of the College of Cardinals and a papal legate. To him ecclesiastical offices were simply a source of revenue.

After having been a fugitive under one pope, he became commander-in-chief of the army of Julius II, when during battle at Ravenna, he was defeated and captured by the French. Leo escaped at Milan, and returned to Florence, where Pope Julius II had just died. By shrewd bargaining with his fellow cardinals, Leo was able to gain the papal chair.

Leo, as pope, at the onset of the Protestant Revolution, spent large sums of money on architecture, sculpture, and painting, for which he employed such masters as Raphael and Michelangelo. He also spent lavishly on enriching the Vatican library, but he squandered vastly more on the most luxurious and licentious court of Europe and on schemes for the political advancement of the Medici family.

His enormous expenditures led to the shameless practice of selling indulgences. There were widespread protests, but Leo regarded these of small importance, being utterly incapable of realizing the seriousness of the demands and the determination of Luther

The Romans were disgusted when Hadrian VI was chosen to succeed Leo in 1521. They had no desire to undergo an austere reform such as Hadrian appeared to advocate, and a bitter reception awaited him at the papal office. The luxurious Italian nobles had monopolized the office so long that they resented the intrusion of the lowly Dutchman standing against the licentious and luxurious life that had become customary at the Vatican.

Hadrian's attempts to bring about some reforming measures brought upon him vile slander and threats of assassinations and poisonings, but if Hadrian had been supported by the cardinals and the King of France, and if he had been given a few more years, he may well have been able to introduce such reforms in clerical and monastic life and in the administration of the church that would have greatly lessened the force of Lutheran criticism and checked the progress of the revolution. However, neither the emperor nor the king of France would offer support that he needed, and he died after only two years in office.

Clement VII, pope 1523-1534, utterly failed to carry forward any reforms attempted by Hadrian. Like Leo X, he was devoid of interest in matters of religion and was concerned chiefly with the advancement of the political interests of his family. His usual scheme was to secure favors from both the emperor and the king of France by double-dealing, without allowing the influence of either to become too powerful in Italy. The three-way conflict that existed was greatly in favor of the growth of Protestantism.

Paul III, who was pope from 1534 to 1549, was in his tastes and principles much like Leo and Clement, but he vastly surpassed them in diplomatic skill and political insight. He had come to fully realize the seriousness of the ecclesiastical situation and sought to strengthen his ability to govern by the appointment of several of the ablest Church statesmen in Italy to help carry out his plans. His appointments included a zealous reformer who stood for compromise and conciliation with Protestantism, a Catholic zealot who had become dedicated to the Spanish idea of reform through inquisition, and diplomats to press for his interests in England and to strive with Calvin for dominance in Geneva.

Paul was grossly immoral, but he professed to have the reformation of the Church at heart. He came to realize that because of neglect by the previous popes, the Church had suffered enormous loss in territory and influence and had failed to check the progress of the Protestant Revolution. After failure of negotiations with the Protestants, as advised by his counselors, he adopted a policy of uncompromising hostility toward every form of Protestantism. The tool for his program would be a Spanish-type inquisition, led by the Jesuits, and decrees issues through a general *Council.*

PLANS FOR A GENERAL COUNCIL

Luther and the German princes who protected the Lutheran movement had long demanded that the Lutheran cause be judged by a general council. They further demanded that it be free from papal control and that Scripture be the only authority for doctrine and practice. The need for reform continued to grow and came to be shared, not only among Luther's followers, but among many of the established Church, as well.

German princes and leading men, both Catholic and Protestant, were opposed to any council to be held in Italy, and they agreed to have nothing to do with a council to be presided over by a pope. Nevertheless, Paul III proceeded to issue orders on two separate occasions, without success, for a council to be held in Northern Italy. The fact that he received no favorable response indicates the lowly state of papal authority at the time. The papacy had deservedly lost the favor of its own people by reason of corruption.

The pope and the emperor conferred personally and chose Trent, an Austrian city only a few miles from the Italian border, to be the site of the council, but war broke out between the emperor and the king of France, and nothing could be done until the war was over. When a peace treaty was made between them, both, parties agreed to cooperate in the council. Accordingly, the pope issued a new order calling for the council to assemble in Trent in March, 1545.

A great difficulty in securing cooperation between the papal and imperial parties was to agree upon the work to be attempted. The emperor had at heart the reunion of western Christendom as a means of strengthening the imperial power against Turkish invasion and putting to an end the ruinous internal strife occasioned by the Protestant Revolution. Recognizing the corruption and abuses in the Church, he felt the absolute necessity of reform, in order to lead to the conciliation of all who were not yet beyond hope.

On the other hand, due to the fact that Catholic doctrine had never been set forth completely by the Church, it was of fundamental importance to the pope that exact definition of the doctrines of the Church be fully expressed. Most of the earlier councils had been occupied with individual doctrines, and a great diversity of doctrines had been approved. The time had come, he thought, for the inquisitors of heresy to know precisely what the Church taught and precisely what errors were outside of the pale of toleration. His policy, and the policy of the Church, would not be to win the favor of the Protestants by correcting abuses, but to cut off Protestantism from fellowship.

The emperor and the pope agreed that both the reformation and the definition of the doctrines should be attempted, but it took a little longer to establish the order of precedence. Papal spokesmen nervously suggested that reformation was a delicate matter to be approached cautiously, for great harm might be done in attempting to abolish traditional and deep-seated abuses. Therefore it should be attempted only after the settlement of the doctrinal statements.

The emperor's party demanded that the settlement of doctrine await its turn. It was finally agreed that two separate departments would be entrusted to work at the same time on the two plans, and that alternate sessions of the Council would be devoted to each.

THE COUNCIL OF TRENT

Seven sessions of the Council were held at Trent from March, 1545 to March 1547, when pestilence broke out due to improper sanitation. Dissension between the parties and the ill health and death of the pope prevented assembly until 1551, when under Julius III (pope from 1550-1555) the Council continued with its work for about a year. A number of Protestant ambassadors were present in response to the invitation of the emperor, who had assured them of the right to deliver their opinions freely, but it became more and more evident that they could hope for no advantage from a council whose chief business was to exterminate them, and that any reforms would be insignificant.

In 1552, war broke out again between the emperor and the Protestant princes of Germany, leading once more to the suspension of the Council. The French, not wishing the emperor to become too powerful, assisted the Protestants against the emperor and forced him to come to terms and to officially end the war, by means of The *Peace of Augsburg* in 1555.

The treaty, without the involvement of the pope, gave the prince of each territory the right to freely choose between the Roman form of Christianity and Lutheranism as the religion of his realm. Unlimited power was given to each prince over the conscience of all his subjects, but people found in a territory of the opposing religion were to be given time to sell their effects and to move to another territory. There were no provisions for the rights of Calvinists or any other dissenters, a feature which made future conflict inevitable.

The deaths of two popes in rapid succession, along with certain other problems, prevented further meetings of the council until 1561. It reassembled under Pius IV and continued with only slight interruption until 1564, when its work was completed.

In response to demands for reform, the council made some provision for a better trained clergy; to prevent interference of monks with the local ministry, a license bestowed upon them by medieval popes, persons holding multiple benefices; the appointment of disreputable and incompetent men to ecclesiastical positions, and a higher standard of morality among the clergy. Further, it was required that appointments to the higher positions go to those of good birth, good morals, and be at least fourteen years of age.

While these appear to be commendable reforms, the prospect of their observance was greatly weakened by the clear provision that the authority of the Apostolic See was not affected thereby. From that time forward, the power of dispensation was freely used to greatly reduce the effect of the reforms.

The council considered its attention to doctrine a far more serious matter than that of reform, and formulated its doctrinal decisions into canons and decrees. The decrees were the statements of the Roman dogma that must be believed. Each was followed by a canon, which was a condemnation of contrary views, and each concluded with an anathema. The canons systematically anathematized the teachings of Lutheranism, Calvinism, and other reformatory groups, and the last act of the council was the pronouncement of a double curse upon all heretics.[69]

The *Congregation of the Council* was established as a department of the papal office to provide authoritative interpretation, and the infallible head of the church would have the last word in all disputes. *The Canons and Dogmatic Decrees of the Council of Trent*[70] was signed by 255 "fathers," and was solemnly confirmed by Pius IV in 1564.

Far from being truly ecumenical (or representing all Christianity), as it claimed to be, the Council of Trent was simply a Roman Synod, where neither the Protestants nor the Greek Church was represented. The Greeks were never invited, and the Protestants were condemned without a hearing. For the Latin Church, however, it was an exceedingly important and historical clerical assembly. It completed the doctrinal system of medieval Catholicism, with the exception of a few controversial articles, and placed the stamp of Romanism upon it. It also settled its relationship to Protestantism, which it thrust out of its bosom with the solemnity of an anathema.[71]

By the time the *Canons and Decrees* was published, the Jesuits were thoroughly in control of the policy of the Church, and without regard for the provisions of the

---

[69] Schaff, I, 94.
[70] *The Canons and Dogmatic Decrees of the Council of Trent* is reproduced in Schaff,, Vol.. II, p. 77 .
[71] Schaff, II, 95.

Peace of Augsburg, they were ready to carry out their ruthless policy of inquisition.

THE THIRTY YEARS' WAR

Some of the earlier wars of the period of the Reformation have been discussed, but those were only the beginning of horrors. The *Peace of Augsburg* gave Lutherans the right to exist, but no such accommodation was given to Calvinism or any other group. It gave the prince unlimited power over the consciences of his subjects, whose rights were protected only to the extent of being able to sell their belongings and leave the territory of the prince. The treaty, therefore, only postponed the wars that were inevitable. *The Canons and Decrees of the Council of Trent* contained the marching orders for the war on heresy and defined the doctrines that stood beyond the pale of toleration of the Roman Church.

PROVOCATIONS FOR WAR

Ferdinand, a member of the Hapsburg family, was brought up strongly under the influence of the Jesuits and was an enthusiastic supporter of the Church. From 1596 to 1617, as Archduke of Styria, a duchy in Austria, he carried out remorselessly the Jesuit policy in which he had been schooled from infancy, prohibiting Protestant worship, banishing Protestant clergy, and forcing the heretics to choose between exile and conversion.

Maximillian, King of Bavaria, also favored the Jesuit plan. While applying these brutal measures, he became involved in the gross violation of the *Peace of Augsburg* by his actions against Donauworth, a Lutheran independent imperial city, under the direct authority of the emperor. The city was on the border of Maximilian's domains and near the province of the Bishop of Augsburg. To guard itself against being overwhelmed by its Roman Catholic neighbors, the city had made use of its right under the *Peace of Augsburg* to exclude Catholics, but agreed to tolerate a monastery on the express condition that its inmates should make no demonstration outside the walls.

In 1607, the monks were encouraged by outside parties to violate the understanding and were roughly handled by the Protestant population. The rough treatment by the Protestants furnished a pretext for Maximilian to lay the matter before Emperor Rudolph II, also a member of the Hapsburg family.

Rudolph agreed with the Jesuits' policy of inquisition. He put the city under the imperial ban and gave Maximilian the right to deal with the population as he pleased. Maximilian invaded the city, established Catholic worship in the churches, quartered the soldiers on the people for the purpose of converting them to the Catholic faith, and held the city responsible for his expenses.

The aggressiveness and rigor with which Ferdinand and Maximilian carried out their policies thoroughly alarmed the Protestant electors (princes entitled to elect the emperor) and resulted in forming an Evangelical Union in 1609. The Elector of Saxony and the Landgrave (or Count) of Hesse-Cassel, however, maintained a hostile attitude toward the Union. Apparently, the Elector of Saxony hoped to secure for himself certain territories for his cooperation with the Catholics. In response to the organization of the Union, the Roman Catholic princes promptly organized the Holy League.

About the same time, there were other troubles brewing. Emperor Rudolf II attempted to suppress the

Protestants in Bohemia and some neighboring states, which brought about a great uprising of the Protestants and the granting of the Royal Charter (1609), granting full religious liberty.

An even more explosive situation developed when the Duke of Cleves (a territory bordering the Protestant Netherlands) died without issue, leaving nine or more claimants to succession. Emperor Rudolph II sent Archduke Leopold to take possession of the territory in the name of the emperor, but the two Lutheran Claimants joined hands in opposition to the common enemy, and war broke out with several powers, both Catholic and Protestant taking part.

Henry IV, of France, sent a large army to support the Lutherans, hoping to strike a decisive blow against the growing threat of the House of Austria, but Henry was assassinated by a Jesuit, and the emperor was too busy with the war in Hungary and Bohemia to back up his claims. With the aid of France and the United Netherlands, the two Lutheran claimants were left to divide the territory between themselves, but the dispute came very near to touching off an all-out war.

It was a tragedy for the Protestants when Ferdinand of Styria succeeded the throne as king of Bohemia and Hungary in 1617. Even though Ferdinand had allowed himself to sign the Royal Charter guaranteeing liberties for the Bohemian Protestants, they had not long to wait to feel his oppressive hand, for he quickly put into practice his policy of suppression.

The Roman Catholics, with Ferdinand's connivance, began to refuse Protestants the use of certain churches in the royal domains, contrary to a charter that guaranteed freedom of worship. Of two buildings they had erected, the Protestants were rigorously excluded from one, and the walls of the other were demolished. Their appeals to both the Church and to the government were treated with contempt.

Under the leadership of a reckless and impetuous German Bohemian, the Protestants decided upon violent resistance. They forced themselves into the apartment of the counselors of the king to demand that the ministers answer directly as to the source of the hateful behavior. When satisfactory answers were not forthcoming they seized two ministers, and following an old Bohemian custom, they through them out of a window, sixty feet, or more, above the moat.

THE OUTBREAK OF WAR (1618)

The Protestant nobles quickly took possession of the city, deposed Ferdinand, and chose Frederick of the Palatinate, a Protestant state in Germany, as the new king of Bohemia. Frederick was the son-in-law of James I, King of England and it was expected that James would furnish aid for the Protestant cause in Bohemia, but James believed in the *Divine Right of kings* and did not approve the dethroning of Ferdinand. James also was negotiating with Spain on the possible marriage of his son, Charles to the daughter of the Spanish king. Therefore, he would do nothing to upset the Catholics.

About the same time, the emperor died, and Frederick could easily have been made emperor except for the jealousy of John George of Saxony, a Lutheran who could not endure to see Frederick succeed in such an ambitious scheme.

Consequently, and utterly disheartening to the Protestants, Ferdinand was elected as the new emperor and proceeded, forthwith, to crush Protestantism in Bohemia and other Austrian dependencies. With the backing of Maximilian of Bavaria, the Spanish armies, and the treasures of Spain, he proceed as far as he could reach across the continent of Europe, and while Frederick was in Austria contending with the armies of Ferdinand and Maximilian, his own Palatinate was being ravaged by the Spanish army.

Following the victory of Ferdinand in the Austrian provinces, the Jesuits were on hand in full force to aid in the ruthless work of extermination. At the beginning of the war, the Protestants constituted eighty percent of the population of Bohemia, and in an incredibly short period of time they were almost gone.

DENMARK TAKES THE LEAD (1625-1629)

The Lutheran princes of northern Germany and the kings of Denmark and Sweden had reason to be alarmed. The ruthless way in which the counter-Reformation was being carried out in Austria and its dependencies opened their eyes to the likelihood that similar methods would soon be used in the North.

After negotiations had broken off between England and Spain concerning royal marriage plans, England was free to deal with other questions. England and France were jealous of the growing power of the emperor and joined together in sending an army to the Palatinate under a General Mansfeld.

Christian IV of Denmark, aided chiefly by Mansfeld, led his armies against the armies of Ferdinand and the Holy League. Unfortunately, much of Protestant Germany was not ready to lend support, while Ferdinand had added a leader of extraordinary military ability to his cause – General Wallenstein, a Bohemian. Christian IV was defeated again and again as the inhabitants of the towns bound themselves by oath to spend the last drop of their blood, if need be, in defending their religion and their liberty, but Christian was finally forced to sign a treaty and withdrew from the field in 1629.

SWEDEN TAKES ITS TURN

Gustavus Adolphus, of Sweden, was sincerely devoted to the cause of Protestantism and realized the danger to Sweden if Ferdinand became too powerful, but he was unwilling to enter into the conflict before he could be sure of his means of success. He knew how to bide his time when the circumstances required patience, but eventually, John George of Saxony saw that his only safety lay in taking up the defense of the Protestants, and the Elector of Brandenburg, the Margrave of Hesse-Cassel, and many less influential nobles saw themselves compelled to choose between assisting Gustavus Adolphus or giving in to the demands of Ferdinand. They all joined with Gustavus in the conflict, and only then did the fortunes of Protestantism began to rise.

Beginning in 1630, Gustavus was victorious in the Battle of Leipzig and many others, including the battle for Donauworth, which had been cruelly wrested from the Protestants a few years earlier by Maximilian. Before the end of 1631, all of Germany, except the hereditary possessions of the house of Austria, was under the control of the Swedish king, and John George of Saxony took Bohemia almost without resistance.

There seemed to be no limit to what Gustavus could accomplish, but on Noveber17,1632,[72] Wallenstein was strongly entrenched and had great advantage as the two greatest soldiers of the age were now arrayed against each other. Gustavus attacked, but for some unknown reason had refused to put on his armor. As he

---

[72]Date given by Boak,II, 82. (Newman gives Nov. 16, 1633).

waved his sword to move forward and charged toward the enemy, he looked heavenward saying, "Now, in God's name, Jesus, give us today to fight for the honor of thy holy name." Gustavus went forward to his death, but the victory was won.

Just as the Protestant cause seemed to be triumphant, the only man who could command the Protestant forces was taken away. The victory had been gained at too great a price. The Swedish army continued to fight until early in 1634, but it was then destroyed in the Battle of Nordlingen, in Bavaria.

FRANCE ENTERS THE STRUGGLE (1635)

When Cardinal Richelieu came into power as prime minister under Louis XIII, he saw the war as a way to bring glory to France. While he had no sympathy with Protestantism, and would do what he could for its destruction in France, he preferred that Germany be Protestant rather than have the interests of France jeopardized by the Spanish and Austrian branches of the house of Hapsburg.

In 1635, a French army was sent into Germany to join a new Swedish army. From that time forward Richelieu would be regarded as a major participant in the conflict, and the religious character of the war was overshadowed by political interests. With the help of the French, the Protestants were victorious in a long series of campaigns, but by 1643 the determination for the waging of war was well nigh burned out. By 1644 negotiations had begun all across the continent in response to a universal longing for peace.

THE PEACE OF WESTPHLIA, 1648

The situation was so complicated and the many conflicting demands were so deeply entrenched that it was a discouraging task for those who were trying to settle the issues. To settle one of the greatest questions, the year 1627 was fixed as the date of reckoning for the ownership of Church property, an action which left the northern bishoprics in the hands of the Protestants. When, in 1648, all issues were finally settled, one of the most destructive wars in history was finally brought to an end by one of the most influential treaties ever made.

The *Peace of Westphalia* was "a peace Christian, universal, and perpetual, and a friendship true and sincere." The universal and profound joy with which the peace was greeted can scarcely be appreciated unless we are able to realize the horrors of the war. Protestants and Catholics, alike, had been taught that nothing could be gained by violent efforts to exterminate one another. Both parties had come to the enlightened conclusion that it would be better to allow one another to live.

The religious settlement, made without the approval of the pope, was much like that of the *Peace of Augsburg*, except that it was far more definite and made full provision for the recognition of Calvinism, as well as Lutheranism, but once again, it belonged to the prince of each province to determine the religion of his subjects and to tolerate or exclude dissenting parties according to his own good pleasure.

POSTSCRIPT

All Europe had been awakened by new light and new learning, but the bright hopes of the Gospel were dimmed as the "Old Evangelical Christianity" gave way to new political movements as they looked for solutions for the problem of religious tyranny. Reforming parties arose who echoed the view of the Established Church that government is a proper institution to promote religion and enforce its practice.

The existence of two opposing parties, each adamant in its own opinions, and each pressing the governmental powers to enforce its teachings, set the stage for warfare and destruction that would bring about unimaginable human suffering for years to come.

The prospect of a different outcome was laid to rest by the nature of the decision-makers on both sides. The reforming parties that arose to bring about reform were just as political in nature and just as intolerant of opposing views as were those of the established church.

When the Peace of Westphalia brought the religious wars to a close in 1648, it marked a time in history when professed Christians were so weary of mutual extermination that they were at last ready for mutual toleration. The Peace, though ending widespread warfare for a time, did not mean that brotherly love would be the rule, nor that freedom of religion would be a consideration. It meant only that other expressions of ill will just as contrary to the spirit of the Gospel would long prevail. The barbaric urge for revenge and the heathen notion that

God would have his will forced upon a people would override all prospects for peace on this earth.

We, along with our institutions that have followed in the wake of the reforming parties, have changed little. Pursuit of political power is not easy to give up, and we can't overcome our longing for the title of "Favored and Official Religion." There seems to be little concern for the significant drift from the nature of the "Old Evangelical Christianity," and hardly a thought is given to the grievous departure from the nature of the New Testament church, itself, whose propounders went forth in Christ's name to proclaim a kingdom "not of this world."

BIBLIOGRAPHY

Boak, Hyma, and Slosson, *The Growth of European Civilization*, 3rd ed. New York: F.S. Crofts & Co., 1938.

The Century Bible (Commentary); *The Acts, Romans;* London: The Caxton Publishing Company.

Conner, W. T., *The Gospel of Redemption* (Nashville, Tenn.), 1945.

Rogers, A.K., *A Student's History of Philosophy,* 3rd ed., New York: The McMillan Company, 1932.

Schaff, Philip, *The Creeds of Christendom, 3 Vols. New York: Harper, 1877.*

Woolley, C. Leonard, *The Sumerians,* New York, W. W. Norton, n.d.

Made in the USA
Charleston, SC
10 November 2012